William Hurrell Mallock

The new Paul and Virginia

Positivism on an island

William Hurrell Mallock

The new Paul and Virginia
Positivism on an island

ISBN/EAN: 9783744722230

Printed in Europe, USA, Canada, Australia, Japan

Cover: Foto ©Andreas Hilbeck / pixelio.de

More available books at **www.hansebooks.com**

THE NEW PAUL AND VIRGINIA

OR

Positivism on an Island

BY

W. H. MALLOCK

AUTHOR OF 'THE NEW REPUBLIC' ETC.

A NEW EDITION

London

CHATTO & WINDUS, PICCADILLY

1890

' Pessimism as to the essential dignity of man is one of the surest marks of the enervating influence of this dream of a celestial glory'

Mr Frederic Harrison

'Those who can read the signs of the times read in them
that the kingdom of man is at hand '— Professor CLIFFORD

Thou art smitten, O God, thou art smitten ; thy curse is
    upon thee, O Lord !
And the love song of earth as thou diest, resounds through
    the wind of its wings,
Glory to man in the highest, for man is the master of
    things

Songs before Sunrise

CONTENTS.

THE

NEW PAUL AND VIRGINIA.

CHAPTER I.

THE magnificent ocean-steamer the *Australasian* was bound for England, on her homeward voyage from Melbourne, carrying Her Majesty's mails and ninety-eight first-class passengers. Never did vessel start under happier auspices. The skies were cloudless; the sea was smooth as glass. There was not a sound of sickness to

B

be heard anywhere; and when dinner-
time came there was not a single ab-
sentee nor an appetite wanting

But the passengers soon discovered
they were lucky in more than weather.
Dinner was hardly half over before two
of the company had begun to attract
general attention; and every one all
round the table was wondering, in whis-
pers, who they could possibly be.

One of the objects of this delightful
curiosity was a large-boned, middle-aged
man, with gleaming spectacles, and lank,
untidy hair; whose coat fitted him so ill,
and who held his head so high, that
one saw at a glance he was some great
celebrity.   The other was a beautiful lady

of about thirty years of age, the like of whom nobody present had ever seen before. She had the fairest hair and the darkest eyebrows, the largest eyes and the smallest waist conceivable; art and nature had been plainly struggling as to which should do the most for her; whilst her bearing was so haughty and distinguished, her glance so tender, and her dress so expensive and so fascinating, that she seemed at the same time to defy and to court attention.

Evening fell on the ship with a soft warm witchery. The air grew purple, and the waves began to glitter in the moonlight. The passengers gathered in knots upon the deck, and the distinguished strangers were still the subject of conjecture. At last the secret was discovered by the wife of an old colonial judge ; and the news spread like wildfire. In a few minutes all knew that there were on board the *Australasian* no less personages than Professor Paul Darnley and the superb Virginia St. John.

CHAPTER II.

MISS ST. JOHN had, for at least six years, been the most renowned woman in Europe. In Paris and St. Petersburg, no less than in London, her name was equally familiar both to princes and to pot-boys ; indeed, the gaze of all the world was fixed on her. Yet, in spite of this exposed situation, scandal had proved powerless to wrong her ; she defied detraction. Her enemies could but echo her friends' praise

of her beauty; her friends could but con-
firm her enemies' description of her character. Though of birth that might almost
be called humble, she had been connected
with the heads of many distinguished
families; and so general was the affection
she inspired, and so winning the ways
in which she contrived to retain it, that
she found herself, at the age of thirty,
mistress of nothing except a large fortune. She was now converted with sur-
prising rapidity by a Ritualistic priest, and
she became in a few months a model
of piety and devotion. She made lace
trimmings for the curate's vestments;
she bowed at church as often and pro-
foundly as possible; she enjoyed nothing

so much as going to confession; she learnt to despise the world. Indeed, such utter dross did her riches now seem to her, that, despite all the arguments of her ghostly counsellor, she remained con-vinced that they were far too worthless to offer to the Church, and she saw nothing for it but to still keep them for herself. The mingled humility and discretion of this resolve so won the heart of a gifted colonial bishop, then on a visit to England, that, having first assured himself that Miss St. John was sincere in making it, he besought her to share with him his humble mitre, and make him the happiest prelate in the whole Catholic Church. Miss St. John consented. The

nuptials were celebrated with the most
elaborate ritual, and after a short honey-
moon the bishop departed for his South
Pacific diocese of the Chasuble Islands,
to prepare a home for his bride, who
was to follow him by the next steamer.

Professor Paul Darnley, in his own
walk of life, was even more famous
than Virginia had been in hers. He had
written three volumes on the origin of
life, which he had spent seven years in
looking for in infusions of hay and cheese;
he had written five volumes on the en-
tozoa of the pig, and two volumes of
lectures, as a corollary to these, on the
sublimity of human heroism and the
whole duty of man. He was renowned

all over Europe and America as a complete embodiment of enlightened modern thought. He criticised everything ; he took nothing on trust, except the unspeakable sublimity of the human race and its august terrestrial destinies. And, in his double capacity of a seer and a *savant*, he had destroyed all that the world had believed in the past, and revealed to it all that it is going to feel in the future. His mind indeed was like a sea, into which the other great minds of the age discharged themselves, and in which all the slight discrepancies of the philosophy of the present century mingled together and formed one harmonious whole. Nor was he less successful in his own private life. He married, at the age of forty, an excellent evangelical lady, ten years his senior, who wore a green gown, grey corkscrew curls, and who had a fortune of two hundred thousand pounds. Deeply pledged though she was to the most vapid figments of Christianity, Mrs. Darnley was yet proud beyond measure of her husband's world-wide fame, for she did but imperfectly understand the grounds of it. Indeed, the only thing that marred her happiness was the single tenet of his that she had really mastered. This, unluckily, was that he disbelieved in hell. And so, as Mrs. Darnley conceived that that place was designed mainly to hold those who doubted its existence, she daily talked her utmost and left no text unturned to convince her darling of his very dangerous error. These assiduous arguments soon began to tell. The Professor grew moody and brooding, and he at last suggested to his medical man that a voyage round the world, unaccompanied by his wife, was the prescription most needed by his failing patience. Mrs. Darnley at length consented with a fairly good grace. She made her husband pledge himself that he would hot be absent for above a twelvemonth, or else, she said, she should immediately come after him. She bade him the tenderest of adieus, and promised to pray till his return for his recovery of a faith in hell.

The Professor, who had but exceeded his time by six months, was now on board the *Australasian*, homeward bound to his wife. Virginia was outward bound to her husband.

CHAPTER III.

HE sensation created by the presence of these two celebrities was profound beyond description; and the passengers were never weary of watching the gleaming spectacles and the square-toed boots of the one, and the liquid eyes and the ravishing toilettes of the other. Virginia's acquaintance was made almost instantly by three pale-faced curates, and so well did their friendship prosper, that they soon sang at nightfall with her a beautiful vesper hymn. Nor did the matter end here, for the strains sounded so lovely, and Virginia looked so devotional, that most of the passengers the night after joined in a repetition of this touching evening office.

The Professor, as was natural, held quite aloof, and pondered over a new species of bug, which he had found very plentiful in his berth. But it soon occurred to him that he often heard the name of God being uttered otherwise than in swearing. He listened more attentively to the sounds which he had at first set down as negro-melodies, and he soon became convinced that they were something whose very

existence he despised himself for remembering — namely, Christian hymns.
He then thought of the three curates,
whose existence he despised himself
for remembering also. And the conviction rapidly dawned on him that,
though the passengers seemed fully
alive to his fame as a man of science,
they could yet know very little of all
that science had done for them ; and of
the death-blow it had given to the foul
superstitions of the past. He therefore
resolved that next day he would preach
them a lay-sermon.

At the appointed time the passengers
gathered eagerly round him—all but
Virginia, who retired to her cabin

when she saw that the preacher wore no surplice, as she thought it would be a mortal sin to listen to a sermon without one.

The Professor began amidst a profound silence. He first proclaimed to his hearers the great primary axiom on which all modern thought bases itself. He told them that there was but one order of things—it was so much neater than two ; and if we would be certain of anything, we must never doubt this. Thus, since countless things exist that the senses *can* take account of, it is evident that nothing exists that the senses can *not* take account of. The senses can take no account of God ; therefore God does not exist. Men of science can only see theology in a ridiculous light, therefore theology has no side that is not ridiculous. He then told them a few of the names that enlightened thinkers had applied to the Christian deity—how Professor Tyndall had called him an 'atom-manufacturer,' and Professor Huxley a 'pedantic drill-sergeant.' The passengers at once saw how demonstrably at variance with fact was all religion, and they laughed with a sense of humour that was quite new to them. The Professor's tones then became more solemn, and, having extinguished error, he at once went on to unveil the brilliant light of truth. He showed them how, viewed by modern

c

science, all existence is a chain, with a
gas at one end and no one knows what
at the other; and how Humanity is a
link somewhere; but—holy and awful
thought!—we can none of us tell where.
'However,' he proceeded, 'of one thing
we can be quite certain: all that is, is
matter; the laws of matter are eternal, and we cannot act or think without conforming to them; and if,' he said,
'we would be solemn and high, and
happy, and heroic, and saintly, we have
but to strive and struggle to do what
we cannot for an instant avoid doing.
Yes,' he exclaimed, 'as the sublime
Tyndall tells us, let us struggle to at-
tain to a deeper knowledge of matter,

and a more faithful conformity to its laws !'

The Professor would have proceeded, but the weather had been rapidly growing rough, and he here became violently sea-sick.

'Let us,' he exclaimed hurriedly, 'conform to the laws of matter and go below.'

Nor was the advice premature. A storm arose, exceptional in its suddenness and its fury. It raged for two days without ceasing. The *Australasian* sprang a leak ; her steering gear was disabled ; and it was feared she would go ashore on an island that was seen dimly through the fog to the leeward. The

boats were got in readiness. A quantity
of provisions and of the passengers'
baggage was already stowed in the cut·
ter ; when the clouds parted, the sun
came out again, and the storm subsided
almost as quickly as it rose.

CHAPTER IV.

N O sooner were the ship's damages in a fair way to be repaired than the Professor resumed his sermon. He climbed into the cutter, which was still full of the passengers' baggage, and sat down on the largest of Virginia's boxes. This so alarmed Virginia that she incontinently followed the Professor into the cutter, to keep an eye on her property; but she did not forget to stop her ears with her fingers,

that she might not be guilty of listening
to an unsurpliced minister.

The Professor took up the thread
of his discourse just where he had
broken it off. Every circumstance fa-
voured him. The calm sea was sparkling under the gentlest breeze; all
Nature seemed suffused with gladness;
and at two miles' distance was an enchanting island, green with every kind
of foliage, and glowing with the hues
of a thousand flowers. The Professor,
having reminded his hearers of what
nonsense they now thought all the
Christian teachings, went on to show
them the blessed results of this. Since
the God that we once called all-holy

is a fable, that Humanity is all-holy must be a fact. Since we shall never be sublime, and solemn, and unspeakably happy hereafter, it is evident that we can be sublime, and solemn, and unspeakably happy here. 'This,' said the Professor, 'is the new Gospel. It is founded on exact thought. It is the Gospel of the kingdom of man; and had I only here a microscope and a few chemicals, I could demonstrate its eternal truth to you. There is no heaven to seek for; there is no hell to shun. We have nothing to strive and live for except to be unspeakably happy.'

This eloquence was received with enthusiasm. The captain in particular, who had a wife in every port he touched at, was overjoyed at hearing that there was no hell; and he sent for all the crew, that they might learn the good news likewise. But soon the general gladness was marred by a sound of weeping. Three-fourths of the passengers, having had time to reflect a little, began exclaiming that as a matter of fact they were really completely miserable, and that for various reasons they could never be anything else. 'My friends,' said the Professor, quite undaunted, 'that is doubtless completely true. You are not happy now; you probably never will be. But that, I can assure you, is of very little moment. Only conform faithfully to the laws of matter, and your children's children will be happy in the course of a few centuries; and you will like that far, far better than being happy yourselves. Only consider the matter in this light, and you yourselves will in an instant become happy also; and whatever you say, and whatever you do, think only of the effect it will have five hundred years afterwards.'

At these solemn words, the anxious faces grew calm. An awful sense of the responsibility of each one of us, and the infinite consequences of every human act, was filling the hearts of all; when by a faithful conformity to the laws of matter, the boiler blew up, and the *Australasian* went down. In an instant the air was rent with yells and cries; and all the Humanity that was on board the vessel was busy, as the Professor expressed it, uniting itself with the infinite azure of the past. Paul and Virginia, however, floated quietly away in the cutter, together with the baggage and provisions.

Virginia was made almost senseless by the suddenness of the catastrophe; and on seeing five sailors sink within three yards of her, she fainted dead away. The Professor begged her not to take it so much to heart, as these were the very men who had got the cutter in readiness; 'and they are, therefore,' he said, 'still really alive in the fact of our happy escape.' Virginia, however, being quite insensible, the Professor turned to the last human being still to be seen above the waters, and shouted to him not to be afraid of death, as there was certainly no hell, and that his life, no matter how degraded and miserable, had been a glorious mystery, full of infinite significance. The next moment the struggler was snapped up by a shark. Our friends, meanwhile, borne by a current, had been drifting rapidly towards the island. And the Professor, spreading to the breeze Virginia's beautiful lace parasol, soon brought the cutter to the shore on a beach of the softest sand.

CHAPTER V.

THE scene that met Paul's eyes was one of extreme loveliness. He found himself in a little fairy bay, full of translucent waters, and fringed with silvery sands. On either side it was protected by fantastic rocks, and in the middle it opened inland to an enchanting valley, where tall tropical trees made a grateful shade. and where the ground was carpeted with the softest moss and turf.

Paul's first care was for his fair companion. He spread a costly cashmere shawl on the beach, and placed her, still fainting, on this. In a few moments she opened her eyes; but was on the point of fainting again as the horrors of the last half-hour came back to her, when she caught sight in the cutter of the largest of her own boxes, and she began to recover herself. Paul begged her to remain quiet whilst he went to reconnoitre.

He had hardly proceeded twenty yards into the valley, when to his infinite astonishment he came on a charming cottage, built under the shadow of a bread-tree, with a broad verandah, plate-glass windows, and red window-blinds. His first thought was that this could be no desert island at all, but some happy European settlement. But, on approaching the cottage, it proved to be quite untenanted, and from the cob-webs woven across the doorway it seemed to have been long abandoned. Inside there was abundance of luxurious fur niture; the floors were covered with gorgeous Indian carpets; and there was a pantry well stocked with plate and glass and table-linen. The Professor could not tell what to make of it, till, examining the structure more closely, he

found it composed mainly of a ship's
timbers. This seemed to tell its own
tale, and he at once concluded that he
and Virginia were not the first castaways
who had been forced to make the island
for some time their dwelling-place.

Overjoyed at this discovery, he hastened back to Virginia. She was by
this time apparently quite recovered,
and was kneeling on the cashmere
shawl, with a rosary in her hands designed especially for the use of Anglo-
Catholics, alternately lifting up her eyes
in gratitude to heaven, and casting them
down in anguish at her torn and
crumpled dress. The poor Professor was
horrified at the sight of a human being

in this degrading attitude of superstition. But as Virginia quitted it with alacrity as soon as ever he told his news to her, he hoped he might soon convert her into a sublime and holy Utilitarian.

The first thing she besought him to do was to carry her biggest box to this charming cottage, that she might change her clothes, and appear in something fit to be seen in. The Professor most obligingly at once did as she asked him ; and whilst she was busy at her toilette, he got from the cutter what provisions he could, and proceeded to lay the table. When all was ready, he rang a gong which he found suspended in the lobby; Virginia appeared shortly in a beautiful pink dressing-gown, embroidered with silver flowers ; and just before sunset the two sat down to a really excellent meal. The bread-tree at the door of the cottage contributed some beautiful French rolls; close at hand also they discovered a butter-tree; and the Professor had produced from the cutter a variety of salt and potted meats, *pâté de foie gras*, cakes, preserved fruits, and some bottles of fine champagne. This last helped much to raise their spirits. Virginia found it very dry, and exactly suited to her palate. She had but drunk five glasses of it, when her natural smile returned to her, though she was much

disappointed because Paul took no no-
tice of her dressing-gown, and when she
had drunk three glasses more she quietly
went to sleep on the sofa.

The moon had by this time risen in
dazzling splendour, and the Professor
went out and lighted a cigar. All
during dinner there had been a feeling
of dull despair in his heart, which even
the champagne did not dissipate. But
now, as he surveyed in the moonlight
the wondrous Paradise in which his
strange fate had cast him, his mood
changed. The air was full of the scents
of a thousand night-smelling flowers;
the sea murmured on the beach in soft,
voluptuous cadences. The Professor's

cigar was excellent. He now saw his situation in a truer light. Here was a bountiful island, where earth unbidden brought forth all her choicest fruits, and most of the luxuries of civilisation . had already been wafted thither. Existence here seemed to be purified from all its evils. Was not this the very condition of things which all the sublimest and exactest thinkers of modern times had been dreaming and lecturing and writing books about for a good half-century? Here was a place where Humanity could do justice to itself, and realise those glorious destinies which all exact thinkers take for granted must be in store for it. True, from the mass of Humanity he was

completely cut away; but Virginia was
his companion. Holiness, and solemnity,
and unspeakably significant happiness did
not, he argued, depend on the multiplica-
tion table. He and Virginia represented
Humanity as well as a million couples.
They were a complete humanity in themselves, and humanity in a perfectible
shape; and the very next day they would
make preparations for fulfilling their holy
destiny, and being as solemnly and unspeakably happy as it was their stern
duty to be.

The Professor turned his eyes up-
wards to the starry heavens, and a
sense came over him of the eternity and
the immensity of Nature, and the de-

monstrable absence of any intelligence that guided it. These reflections naturally brought home to him with more vividness the stupendous and boundless importance of Man. His bosom swelled violently, and he cried aloud, his eyes still fixed on the firmament, ' Oh, important All! oh, important Me!'

When he came back to the cottage he found Virginia just getting off the sofa, and preparing to go to bed. She was too sleepy even to say goodnight to him, and with evident want of temper was tugging at the buttons of her dressing-gown. 'Ah!' she murmured as she left the room, 'if God, in His infinite mercy, had only spared my maid!'

Virginia's evident discontent gave profound pain to Paul. 'How solemn,' he exclaimed, 'for half Humanity to be discontented!' But he was still more disturbed at the appeal to a chimerical manufacturer of atoms; and he groaned in tones of yet more sonorous sorrow, 'How solemn for half Humanity to be sunk lower than the beasts by superstition!'

However, he hoped that these stupendous evils might, under the present favourable conditions, vanish in the course of a few days' progress; and he went to bed, full of august auguries.

CHAPTER VI.

NEXT morning he was up be-
times; and the prospects of
Humanity looked more glo-
rious than ever. He gathered some of
the finest pats from the butter-tree, and
some fresh French rolls from the bread-
tree. He discovered a cow close at hand,
that allowed him at once to milk it;
and a little roast pig ran up to him out
of the underwood, and fawning on him
with its trotters, said, 'Come, eat me.'

The Professor vivisected it before Virginia's door, that its automatic noise,
which the vulgar call cries of pain, might
awaken her; and he then set it in a hot
dish on the table.

'It has come! it has come!' he
shouted, rapturously, as Virginia entered
the room, this time in a blue silk dressing-
gown, embroidered with flowers of gold.

'What has come?' said Virginia, pet-
tishly, for she was suffering from a terrible
headache, and the Professor's loud voice
annoyed her. 'You don't mean to say
that we are rescued, are we?'

'Yes,' answered Paul, solemnly; 'we
are rescued. We are rescued from all
the pains and imperfections of a world

that has not learnt how to conform to the laws of matter, and is but imperfectly acquainted with the science of sociology. It is therefore inevitable that, the evils of existence being thus removed, we shall both be solemnly, stupendously, and unspeakably happy.'

' Nonsense!' said Virginia, snappishly, who thought the Professor was joking.

' It is not nonsense,' said the Professor. ' It is deducible from the teachings of John Stuart Mill, of Auguste Comte, of Mr. Frederic Harrison, and of all the exact thinkers who have cast off superstition, and who adore Humanity.'

Virginia meanwhile ate *pâté de foie gras*, of which she was passionately fond;

and, growing a little less sullen, she at
last admitted that they were lucky in
having at least the necessaries of life left
to them.   'But as for happiness—there
is nothing to do here, there is no church
to go to, and you don't seem to care a
bit for my dressing-gown.   What have
we got to make us happy ? '

'Humanity,' replied the Professor
eagerly,—'Humanity, that divine entity,
which is necessarily capable of everything
that is fine and invaluable, and is the
object of indescribable emotion to all
exact thinkers.   And what is Humanity?'
he went on more earnestly; 'you and I
are Humanity—you and I are that august
existence.   You already are all the world

to me ; and I very soon shall be all the world to you. Adored being, it will be my mission and my glory to compel·you to live for me. And then, as modern philosophy can demonstrate, we shall both of us be significantly and unspeakably happy.'

For a few moments Virginia merely stared at Paul. Suddenly she turned quite pale, her lips quivered, and exclaiming, 'How dare you !—and I, too, the wife of a bishop !' she left the room in hysterics.

The Professor could make nothing of this. Though he had dissected many dead women, he knew very little of the hearts of live ones. A sense of shyness

overpowered him, and he felt embar-
rassed, he could not tell why, at being
thus left alone with Virginia.   He lit a
cigar and went out.   Here was a to-do indeed, he thought.   How would progress
be possible if one half of Humanity
misunderstood the other?

He was thus musing, when suddenly
a voice startled him; and in another
moment a man came rushing up to him,
with every demonstration of joy.

'Oh, my dear master! oh, emancipator
of the human intellect! and is it indeed
you?   Thank God!——I beg pardon for
my unspeakable blasphemy — I mean,
thank circumstances over which I have
no control.'

It was one of the three curates, whom Paul had supposed drowned, but who now related how he had managed to swim ashore, despite the extreme length of his black clerical coat. ‘These rags of superstition,’ he said, ‘did their best to drown me. But I survive in spite of them, to covet truth and to reject error. Thanks to your glorious teaching,’ he went on, looking reverentially into the Professor's face, ‘the very notion of an Almighty Father makes me laugh consumedly, it is so absurd and so immoral. Science, through your instrumentality, has opened my eyes. I am now an exact thinker.’

‘Do you believe,’ said Paul, ‘in solemn,

significant, and unspeakably happy Humanity?'

'I do,' said the curate, fervently. 'Whenever I think of Humanity, I groan and moan to myself out of sheer solemnity.'

'Then two thirds of Humanity,' said the Professor, 'are thoroughly enlightened. Progress will now go on smoothly.'

At this moment Virginia came out, having rapidly recovered composure at the sound of a new man's voice.

'You here—you, too!' exclaimed the curate. 'How solemn, how significant! This is truly Providential——I mean this has truly happened through conformity to the laws of matter.'

'Well,' said Virginia, 'since we have a clergyman amongst us, we shall perhaps be able to get on.'

CHAPTER VII.

THINGS now took a better turn. The Professor ceased to feel shy; and proposed, when the curate had finished an enormous breakfast, that they should go down to the cutter, and bring up the things in it to the cottage. 'A few hours' steady progress,' he said, 'and the human race will command all the luxuries of civilisation—the glorious fruits of centuries of onward labour.

The three spent a very busy morning in examining and unpacking the luggage. The Professor found his favourite collection of modern philosophers ; Virginia found a large box of knick-knacks, with which to adorn the cottage; and there was, too, an immense store of wine and of choice provisions.

'It is rather sad,' sighed Virginia, as she dived into a box of French chocolate-creams, 'to think that all the poor people are drowned that these things belonged to.'

'They are not dead,' said the Professor: 'they still live on this holy and stupendous earth. They live in the use we are making of all they had got

E

together. The owner of those chocolate-creams is immortal because you
are eating them.'

Virginia licked her lips and said,
' Nonsense ! '

' It is not nonsense,' said the Professor. ' It is the religion of Humanity.

All day they were busy, and the
time passed pleasantly enough. Wines,
provisions, books, and china ornaments
were carried up to the cottage and
bestowed in proper places. Virginia
filled the glasses in the drawing-room
with gorgeous leaves and flowers and
declared by the evening, as she looked
round her, that she could almost fancy
herself in St. John's Wood.

'See,' said the Professor, 'how rapid is the progress of material civilisation! Humanity is now entering on the fruits of ages. Before long it will be in a position to be unspeakably happy.'

Virginia retired to bed early. The Professor took the curate out with him to look at the stars; and promised to lend him some writings of the modern philosophers, which would make him more perfect in the new view of things. They said good-night, murmuring together that there was certainly no God, that Humanity was very important, and that everything was very solemn.

CHAPTER VIII.

EXT morning the curate began studying a number of essays that the Professor lent him, all written by exact thinkers, who disbelieved in God, and thought Humanity adorable, and most important. Virginia lay on the sofa, and sighed over one of Miss Broughton's novels; and it occurred to the Professor that the island was just the place where, if anywhere, the missing link might be found.

'Ah!' he exclaimed; 'all is still progress. Material progress came to an
end yesterday. Mental progress has
begun to-day. One third of Humanity
is cultivating sentiment; another third
is learning to covet truth. I, the remaining and most enlightened third, will
go and seek it. Glorious, solemn Humanity! I will go and look about for
its arboreal ancestor.'

Every step the Professor took he
found the island more beautiful. But
he came back to luncheon, having been
unsuccessful in his search. Events had
marched quickly in his absence. Virginia was at the beginning of her third
volume; and the curate had skimmed

over so many essays, that he professed himself able to give a thorough ac count of the want of faith that was in him.

After luncheon the three sat together in easy chairs, in the verandah, sometimes talking, sometimes falling into a half-doze.   They all agreed that they were wonderfully comfortable, and the Professor said—

'All Humanity is now at rest, and in utter peace.   It is just taking breath, before it becomes unspeakably and significantly happy.'

He would have said more, but he was here startled by a piteous noise of crying, and the three found themselves confronted by an old woman dripping with sea-water, and with an expression on her face of the utmost misery. They soon recognised her as one of the passengers on the ship. She told them how she had been floated ashore on a spar, and how she had been sustained by a little roast pig, that kindly begged her to eat it, having first lain in her bosom to restore her to warmth. She was now looking for her son.

'And if I cannot find him,' said the old woman, 'I shall never smile again. He has half broken my heart,' she went on, 'by his wicked ways. But if I thought he was dead—dead in the midst of his sins—it would be broken alto-

gether; for in that case he must certainly be in hell.'

'Old woman,' said the Professor,
very slowly and solemnly, 'be comforted.
I announce to you that your son is
alive.'

'Oh, bless you, sir, for that word!'
cried the old woman. 'But where is
he? Have you seen him? Are you
sure that he is living?'

'I am sure of it,' said the Professor,
'because enlightened thought shows me
that he cannot be anything else. It is
true that I saw him sink for a third
time in the sea, and that he was then
snapped up by a shark. But he is as
much alive as ever in his posthumous

activities. He has made you wretched after him; and that is his future life. Become an exact thinker, and you will see that this is so. Old woman,' added the Professor solemnly, 'old woman, listen to me—*You are your son in hell.*'

At this the old woman flew into a terrible rage.

'In hell, sir!' she exclaimed; 'me in hell!—a poor lone woman like me! How dare you!' And she sank back in a chair and fainted.

'Alas!' said the Professor, 'thus is misery again introduced into the world. A fourth part of Humanity is now miserable.'

The curate answered promptly that

if no restoratives were given her, she would probably die in a few minutes. 'And to let her die,' he said, 'is clearly our solemn duty. It will be for the greatest happiness of the greatest number.'

'No,' said the Professor; 'for our sense of pity would then be wounded, and the happiness of all of us would be marred by that.'

'Excuse me,' said the curate; 'but exact thought shows me that pity for others is but the imagining of their misfortune falling on ourselves. Now, we can none of us imagine ourselves exactly in the old woman's case; therefore it is quite impossible that we can pity her.'

'But,' said the Professor, 'such an act would violate our ideas of justice.'

'You are wrong again,' said the curate, 'for exact thought shows me that the love of justice is nothing but the fear of suffering injustice. If we were to kill strong men, we might naturally fear that strong men would kill us. But whatever we do to fainting old women, we cannot expect that fainting old women will do anything to us in return.'

'Your reasoning cannot be sound,' said the Professor, 'for it would lead to the most horrible conclusions. I will solve the difficulty better. I will make the old woman happy, and therefore fit to live. Old woman,' he exclaimed, 'let me beg you to consider this. You are yourself by your own unhappiness expiating your son's sins. Do but think of that, and you will become unspeakably happy.'

Meanwhile, however, the old woman had died. When the Professor discovered this he was somewhat shocked; but at length with a sudden change of countenance, 'We neither of us did it,' he exclaimed; 'her death is no act of ours. It is part of the eternal not-ourselves that makes for righteousness—righteousness, which is, as we all know, but another name for happiness. Let us adore the event with reverence.'

'Yes,' said the curate, 'we are well rid

of her. She was an immoral old woman,
for happiness is the test of morality, and
she was very unhappy.'

'On the contrary,' said the Professor,
'she was a moral old woman; for she has
made us happy by dying so very oppor-
tunely. Let us speak well of the dead.
Her death has been a holy and a blessed
one. She has conformed to the laws of
matter. Thus is unhappiness destined to
fade out of the world. Quick! let us tie
a bag of shot to all the sorrow and evil
of Humanity, which, after all, is only a
fourth part of it, and let us sink her in
the bay close at hand, that she may
catch lobsters for us.'

CHAPTER IX.

'AT last,' said the Professor, as they began dinner that evening, 'the fulness of time has come. All the evils of Humanity are removed, and progress has come to an end because it can go no further. We have nothing now to do but to be unspeakably and significantly happy.'

The champagne flowed freely. Our friends ate and drank of the best, their spirits rose, and Virginia admitted that

this was really 'jolly.' The sense of
the word pleased the Professor, but its
sound seemed below the gravity of the
occasion; so he begged her to say 'sublime' instead. 'We can make it mean,'
he said, 'just the same, but we prefer it
for the sake of its associations.'

It soon, however, occurred to him that
eating and drinking were hardly delights
sufficient to justify the highest state of
human emotion, and he began to fear he
had been feeling sublime prematurely;
but in another moment he recollected
he was an altruist, and that the secret
of their happiness was not that any one
of them was happy, but that they each
knew the others were.

'Yes, my dear curate, ' said the Professor, 'what I am enjoying is the champagne that you drink, and what you are enjoying is the champagne that I drink. This is altruism ; this is benevolence ; this is the sublime outcome of enlightened modern thought. The pleasures of the table, in themselves, are low and beastly ones ; but if we each of us are only glad because the others are enjoying them, they become holy and glorious beyond description.'

' They do,' cried the curate rapturously, ' indeed they do. I will drink another bottle for your sake. It is sublime !' he said, as he tossed off three glasses. ' It is significant !' he said as

he finished three more. ' Tell me, my
dear, do I look significant ? ' he added,
as he turned to Virginia, and suddenly
tried to crown the general bliss by kissing
her.

Virginia started back, looking fire and
fury at him. The Professor was completely astounded by an occurrence so
unnatural, and exclaimed in a voice of
thunder, ' Morality, sir—remember morality ! How dare you upset that which
Professor Huxley tells us must be for
ever strong enough to hold its own ? '

But the last glass of champagne had
put the curate beyond the reach of exact
thought. He tumbled under the table,
and the Professor carried him off to bed.

F

CHAPTER X.

THE Professor, like most serious thinkers, knew but little of that trifle commonly called 'the world.' He had never kissed any one except his wife; even that he did as seldom as possible; and the curate lying dead drunk was the first glimpse he had of what, *par excellence*, is described as 'life.' But though the scene just recounted was thus a terrible shock to him, in one way it gave him an unlooked-for comfort. He had felt that even yet things were not quite as sublime as they should be. He now saw the reason. 'Of course,' he said, 'existence cannot be perfect so long as one third of Humanity makes a beast of itself. A little more progress must be still necessary.'

He hastened to explain this next morning to Virginia, and begged her not to be alarmed at the curate's. scandalous conduct. 'Immorality,' he said, 'is but a want of success in attaining our own happiness. It is evidently most immoral for the curate to be kissing you ; and therefore kissing you would not really conduce to his happiness. I will convince him of this solemn truth in a very

F 2

few moments. Then the essential dignity of human nature will become at
once apparent, and we shall all of us at
last begin to be unspeakably happy.'

The curate, however, altogether declined to be convinced. He maintained
stoutly that to kiss Virginia would be the
greatest pleasure that Humanity could
offer him. 'And if it is immoral as well
as pleasant,' he added, 'I should like it
all the better.'

At this the Professor gave a terrible
groan ; he dropped almost fainting into
a chair ; he hid his face in his hands ;
and murmured half-articulately, ' Then I
can't tell what to do !' In another instant, however, he recovered himself ; and

fixing a dreadful look on the curate, 'That last statement of yours,' he said, 'cannot be true ; for if it were, it would upset all my theories. It is a fact that can be proved and verified, that if you kissed Virginia it would make you miserable.'

'Pardon me,' said the curate, rapidly moving towards her, 'your notion is a remnant of superstition ; I will explode it by a practical experiment.'

The Professor caught hold of the curate's coat-tails, and forcibly pulled him back into his seat.

'If you dare attempt it,' he said, 'I will kick you soundly; and, shocking, immoral man ! you will feel miserable enough then.'

The curate was a terrible coward, and very weak as well. 'You are a great hulking fellow,' he said, eyeing the Professor; 'and I am of a singularly delicate build. I must, therefore, conform to the laws of matter, and give in.' He said this in a very sulky voice; and, going out of the room, slammed the door after him.

A radiant expression suffused the face of the Professor. 'See,' he said to Virginia, 'the curate's conversion is already half accomplished. In a few hours more he will be rational, he will be moral, he will be solemnly and significantly happy.'

The Professor talked like this to Virginia the whole morning; but in spite of all his arguments, she declined to be comforted. 'It is all very well,' she said, 'whilst you are in the way. But as soon as your back is turned, I know he will be at me again.'

'Will you never,' said Paul, by this time a little irritated, 'will you never listen to exact thought? The curate is now reflecting; and a little reflection must inevitably convince him that he does not really care to kiss you, and that it would give him very little real pleasure to do so.'

'Stuff!' exclaimed Virginia, with a sudden vigour at which the Professor was thunderstruck. 'I can tell you,' she went on, 'that better men than he have borne kicks for my sake; and to kiss me is the only thing that that little man cares about.—What *shall* I do?' she exclaimed, bursting into tears. 'Here is one of you insulting me by trying to kiss me; and the other insulting me by saying that I am not worth being kissed!'

'Ah, me!' groaned the poor Professor in an agony, 'here is one third of Humanity plunged in sorrow; and another third has not yet freed itself from vice. When, when, I wonder, will the sublimity begin?'

CHAPTER XI.

T dinner, however, things wore a more promising aspect. The curate had been so terrified by the Professor's threats, that he hardly dared to so much as look at Virginia; and to make up for it, he drank and drank champagne, till the strings of his tongue were loosed, and he was laughing and chattering at a rate that was quite extraordinary. Virginia, seeing herself thus neglected by the curate, began to fear that, as

Paul said, he really did not so much care to kiss her after all. She, therefore, put on all her most enticing ways; she talked, flirted, and smiled her best, and made her most effective eyes, that the curate might see what a prize was for ever beyond his reach.

This state of affairs seemed full of glorious promise. Virginia's tears were dried, she had never looked so radiant and exquisite before. The curate had foregone every attempt to kiss Virginia, and yet apparently he was happiness itself.; and Paul took him aside, as soon as the meal was over, to congratulate him on the holy state to which exact thought had conducted him. 'You see,'

Paul said, 'what a natural growth the loftiest morality is. Virginia doesn't want to be kissed by you. I should be shocked at your doing so shocking a thing as kissing her. If you kissed her, you would make both of us miserable; and, as a necessary consequence, you would be in an agony likewise; in addition to which, I should inevitably kick you.'

'But,' said the curate, 'suppose I kissed Virginia on the sly,—I merely put this as an hypothesis, remember,—and that in a little while she liked it, what then? She and I would both be happy, and you ought to be happy too, because we were.'

'Idiot!' said the Professor. 'Virginia is another man's wife. Nobody really likes kissing another man's wife; nor do wives ever like kissing any one except their husbands. What they really like is what Professor Huxley calls "the un-defined but bright ideal of the highest good," which, as he says, exact thought shows us is the true end of existence. But, pooh! what is the use of all this talking? You know which way your higher nature calls you; and, of course, unless men believe in God, they cannot help obeying their higher nature.'

'I,' said the curate, 'think the belief in God a degrading superstition; I think every one an imbecile who believes a miracle possible. And yet I do not care two straws about the highest good. What you call my lower nature is far the strongest : I mean to follow it to the best of my ability ; and I prefer calling it my higher, for the sake of the associations.'

This plunged the Professor in deeper grief than ever. He knew not what to do. He paced up and down the verandah, or about the rooms, and moaned and groaned as if he had a violent toothache. Virginia and the curate asked what was amiss with him. 'I am agonising,' he said, 'for the sake of holy, solemn, unspeakably dignified Humanity.'

The curate, seeing the Professor thus

dejected, by degrees took heart again; and as Virginia still continued her fascinating behaviour to him, he resolved to try and prove to her that, the test of morality being happiness, the most moral thing she could do would be to allow him to kiss her. No sooner had he begun to propound these views, than the Professor gave over his groaning, seized the curate by the collar, and dragged him out of the room with a roughness that nearly throttled him.

'I was but propounding a theory—an opinion,' gasped the curate. 'Surely thought is free. You will not persecute me for my opinions?'

'It is not for your opinions,' said the

Professor, 'but for the horrible effect they might have. Opinions,' he roared, 'can only be tolerated which have no possible consequences. You may promulgate any of those as much as you like; because to do that would be a self-regarding action.'

CHAPTER XII.

'WELL,' said the curate, 'if I may not kiss Virginia, I will drink brandy instead. That will make me happy enough; and then we shall all be radiant.'

He soon put his resolve into practice. He got a bottle of brandy, he sat himself down under a palm-tree, and told the Professor he was going to make an afternoon of it.

'Foolish man!' said the Professor; 'I was never drunk myself, it is true; but I know that to get drunk makes one's head ache horribly. To get drunk is, therefore, horribly immoral; and therefore I cannot permit it.'

'Excuse me,' said the curate; 'it is a self-regarding action. Nobody's head will ache but mine; so that is my own look-out. I have been expelled from school, from college, and from my first curacy for drinking. So I know well enough the balance of pains and pleasures.'

Here he pulled out his brandy bottle, and applied his lips to it.

G

'Oh, Humanity !' he exclaimed, 'how solemn this brandy tastes !'

Matters went on like this for several days. The curate was too much frightened to again approach Virginia. Virginia at last became convinced that he did not care about kissing her. Her vanity was wounded, and she became sullen ; and this made the Professor sullen also. In fact, two thirds of Humanity were overcast with gloom. The only happy section of it was the curate, who alternately smoked and drank all day long.

'The nasty little beast !' said Virginia to the Professor; 'he is nearly always drunk. I am beginning quite to like

you, Paul, by comparison with him. Let
us turn him out, and not let him live in
the cottage.'

'No,' said the Professor ; 'for he is
one third of Humanity. You do not
properly appreciate the solidarity of mankind. His existence, however, I admit
is a great difficulty.'

One day at dinner-time, shortly afterwards, Paul came in radiant.

'Oh holy, oh happy event!' he exclaimed ; 'all will go right at last.'

Virginia inquired anxiously what had
happened, and Paul informed her that
the curate, who had got more drunk
than usual that afternoon, had fallen
over a cliff, and been dashed to pieces.

'What event,' he asked, 'could be more charming—more unspeakably holy? It bears about it every mark of sanctity. It is for the greatest happiness of the greatest number. Come,' he continued, 'let you and me together, purged of sin, and purged of sorrow as we are—let us begin our love-feast. Let us each seek the happiness of the other. Let us instantly be sublime and happy.'

CHAPTER XIII.

'HE supreme moment is come,' said Paul solemnly, as they sat down to dinner. 'Let us prepare ourselves for realising to the full the essential dignity of Humanity—that *grand être*, which has come, in the course of progress, to consist of you and me. Virginia, consider this. Every condition of happiness that modern thinkers have dreamed of is now fulfilled. We have but to seek each the happiness of the other, and we shall both be in a solemn, a significant, and unspeakable state of rapture. See, here is an exquisite leg of mutton. I,' said Paul, who liked the fat best, ' will give up all the fat to you.'

' And I,' said Virginia, resignedly, ' will give up all the lean to you.'

A few mouthfuls made Virginia feel sick. ' I confess,' said she, ' I can't get on with this fat.'

' I confess,' the Professor answered, ' I don't exactly like this lean.'

' Then let us,' said Virginia, ' be like Jack Sprat and his wife.'

' No,' said the Professor, meditatively, ' that is quite inadmissible. For in that case we should be egoistic hedonists.

However, for to-day it shall be as you say. I will think of something better to-morrow.'

Next day he and Virginia had a chicken apiece; only Virginia's was put before Paul, and Paul's before Virginia; and they each walked round the table to supply each other with the slightest necessaries.

'Ah!' cried Paul, 'this is altruism indeed. I think already I can feel the sublimity beginning.'

Virginia liked this rather better. But soon she committed the sin of taking for herself the liver of Paul's chicken. As soon as she had eaten the whole of it her conscience began to smite her. She confessed her sin to Paul, and inquired, with some anxiety, if he thought she would go to hell for it. ' Metaphorically,' said Paul, 'you have already done so. You are punished by the loss of the pleasure you would have had in giving that liver to me, and also by your know-ledge of my knowledge of your folly in foregoing the pleasure.'

Virginia was much relieved by this answer ; she at once took several more of the Professor's choicest bits, and was happy in the thought that her sins were expiated in the very act of their com-mission, by the latent pain she felt per-suaded they were attended by. . Feeling that this was sufficient, she took care

not to add Paul's disapproval to her
punishment, so she never told him again.

For a short time this practice of altruism seemed to Virginia to have many
advantages. But though the Professor
was always exclaiming, ' How significant
is human life by the very nature of its
constitution!' she very soon found it a
trifle dull. Luckily, however, she hit
upon a new method of exercising morality, and, as the Professor fully admitted, of giving it a yet more solemn
significance.

The Professor having by some acci-
dent lost his razors, his moustaches had
begun to grow profusely, and Virginia had
watched them with a deep but half-con-

scious admiration. At last, in a happy moment, she exclaimed, 'Oh, Paul, do let me wax the ends for you.' Paul at first giggled, blushed, and protested, but, as Virginia assured him it would make her happy, he consented. 'Then,' she said, 'you will know that I am happy, and that in return will make you happy also. Ah!' she exclaimed when the operation was over, 'do go and examine yourself in the glass. I declare you look exactly like Jack Barley—Barley-Sugar, as we used to call him—of the Blues.'

Virginia smiled; suddenly she blushed; the Professor blushed also. To cover the blushes she begged to be allowed to do his hair. 'It will make me so

much happier, Paul,' she said. The
Professor again assented, that he might
make Virginia happy, and that she might
be happy in knowing that he was
happy in promoting her happiness. At
last the Professor, shy and awkward as
he was, was emboldened to offer to do
Virginia's hair in return. She allowed
him to arrange her fringe, and, as she
found he did no great harm to it, she let
him repeat the operation as often as he
liked.

A week thus passed, full, as the Professor said, of infinite solemnity. 'I
admit, Paul,' sighed Virginia, 'that this
altruism, as you call it, is very touching.
I like it very much. But,' she added,

sinking her voice to a whisper, 'are you quite sure, Paul, that it is perfectly moral ?'

'Moral!' echoed the Professor, 'moral! Why, exact thought shows us that it is the very essence of all morality!'

CHAPTER XIV.

MATTERS now went on charmingly. All existence seemed to take a richer colouring, and there was something, Paul said, which, in Professor Tyndall's words, 'gave fulness and tone to it, but which he could neither analyse nor comprehend.' But at last a change came. One morning, whilst Virginia was arranging Paul's moustaches, she was frightened almost into a fit by a sudden apparition at the window. It was a hideous hairy figure, perfectly naked but for a band of silver which it wore about its neck. For a moment it did, nothing but grin and stare; then, uttering a discordant scream, it flung into Virginia's lap a filthy piece of carrion, and in an instant it had bounded away with an almost miraculous activity.

Virginia shrieked with disgust and terror, and clung to Paul's knees for protection. He, however, in some strange way, seemed unmoved and preoccupied. All at once, to her intense surprise, she saw his face light up with an expression of triumphant eagerness. 'The missing link!' he exclaimed, 'the missing link at last! Thank God—I beg pardon for my unspeakable blasphemy—I mean, thank circumstances over which I have no control. I must this instant go out and hunt for it. Give me some pro-- visions in a knapsack, for I will not come back till I have caught it.'

This was a fearful blow to Virginia. She fell at Paul's feet weeping, and besought him in piteous accents that he would not thus abandon her.

'I must,' said the Professor solemnly, 'for I am going in pursuit of Truth. To arrive at Truth is man's perfect and most rapturous happiness. You must surely know that, even if I have forgotten to tell it to you. To pursue truth—holy truth for holy truth's sake—is a more solemn pleasure than even frizzling your hair.'

'Oh,' cried Virginia, hysterically, 'I don't care two straws for truth. What on earth is the good of it?'

'It is its own end,' said the Professor. 'It is its own exceeding great reward. I must be off at once in search of it. Good-bye for the present. Seek truth on your own account, and be unspeakably happy also, because you know that I am seeking it.'

The Professor remained away for three days. For the first two of them Virginia was inconsolable. . She wandered about mournfully with her head dejected. She

very often sighed ; she very often uttered
the name of Paul. At last she surprised
herself by exclaiming aloud to the irre-
sponsive solitude, ' Oh, Paul, until you
were gone, I never knew how passionately
I loved you.' No sooner were these
words out of her mouth than she stood
still, horror-stricken. 'Alas!' she cried,
'and have I really come to this ? I am
in a state of deadly sin, and there is no
priest here to confess to! Alone, alone I
must conquer my forbidden love as I may.
But, ah me, what a guilty thing I am !'

As she uttered these words, her eyes
fell on a tin box of the Professor's, marked
' Private,' which he always kept carefully
locked, and which had before now excited

H

her curiosity. Suddenly she became con-
scious of a new impulse. 'I will pursue
truth! ' she exclaimed. 'I will break
that box open, and I will see what is
inside it. Ah!' she added, as with the
aid of the poker she at last wrenched off
the padlock. 'Paul may be right, after
all. There is more interest in the pursuit of truth than I thought there was.'

The box was full of papers, letters,
and diaries, the greater part of which
were marked 'Strictly private.' Seeing
this, Virginia's appetite for truth became
keener than ever. She instantly began
her researches. The more she read,
the more eager she became; and the
more private appeared the nature of

the documents, the more insatiable did
her thirst for truth grow. To her extreme surprise, she gathered that the
Professor had begun life as a clergyman. There were several photographs of
him in his surplice; and a number of
devout prayers, apparently composed by
himself for his own personal use. This
discovery was the result of her labours.

'Certainly,' she said, 'it is one of
extreme significance. If Paul was a
priest once, he must be a priest now.
Orders are indelible—at least in the
Church of England I know they are.

CHAPTER XV.

AUL came back, to Virginia's extreme relief, without the missing link. But he was still radiant in spite of his failure; for he had discovered, he said, a place where the creature had apparently slept, and he had collected in a card-paper box a large number of its parasites.

'I am glad,' said Virginia, 'that you have not found the missing link: though as to thinking that we really came from monkeys, of course that is too absurd. Now if you could have brought me a nice monkey, I should really have liked that. The Bishop has promised that I shall have a darling one, if I ever reach him—ah me!—if——Paul,' continued Virginia, in a very solemn voice, after a long pause, 'do you know that whilst you have been away I have been pursuing truth? I rather liked it; and I found it very, very significant.'

'Oh, joy!' exclaimed the Professor. 'Oh, unspeakable radiance! Oh, holy, oh essentially dignified Humanity! it will very soon be perfect! Tell me, Virginia, what truths have you been discovering?'

'One truth about you, Paul,' said

Virginia, very gravely, 'and one truth about me. I burn—oh, I burn to tell them to you!'

The Professor was enraptured to hear that one half of Humanity had been thus studying human nature; and he began asking Virginia if her discoveries belonged to the domain of historical or biological science. Meanwhile Virginia had flung herself on her knees before him, and was exclaiming, in piteous accents—

'By my fault, by my own fault, by my very grievous fault, holy father, I confess to you——'

'Is the woman mad?' cried the Professor, starting up from his seat.

'You are a priest, Paul,' said Virginia; 'that is one of the things I have discovered. I am in a state of deadly sin; that is the other: and I must and will confess to you. Once a priest, always a priest. You cannot get rid of your orders, and you must and shall hear me.'

'I was once in orders, it is true,' said Paul, reluctantly; 'but how did you find out my miserable secret?'

'In my zeal for truth,' said Virginia, 'I broke open your tin box; I read all your letters; I looked at your early photographs; I saw all your beautiful prayers.'

'You broke open my box!' cried

the Professor. 'You read my letters and my private papers! Oh, horrible! oh, immoral! What shall we do if one half of Humanity has no feeling of honour?

'Oh!' said Virginia, 'it was all for the love of truth—of solemn and holy truth. I sacrificed every other feeling for that. But I have not told you my truth yet; and I am determined you shall hear it, or I must still remain in my sins. Paul, I am a married woman; and I discover, in spite of that, that I have fallen in love with you. My husband, it is true, is far away; and whatever we do, he could never possibly be the wiser. But I am in a state of mortal sin, nevertheless; and I would give anything in the world if you would only kiss me.'

'Woman!' exclaimed Paul, aghast with fright and horror, 'do you dare to abuse truth, by turning it to such base purposes ?'

'Oh, you are so clever,' Virginia went on, 'and when the ends of your moustaches are waxed, you look positively handsome; and I love you so deeply and so tenderly, that I shall certainly go to hell if you do not give me absolution.'

At this the Professor jumped up, and, staring very hard at Virginia, asked her if, after all that he had said on the ship, she really believed in such ex-

ploded fallacies as hell, God, and priest-
craft.

She reminded him that he had
preached there without a surplice, and
that she had therefore not thought it
right to listen to a word he said.

'Ah!' cried the Professor, with a
sigh of intense relief, 'I see it all now.
How can Humanity ever be unspeakably holy so long as one half of it
grovels in dreams of an unspeakably
holy God? As Mr. Frederic Harrison
truly says, a want of faith in "the essential dignity of man is one of the
surest marks of the enervating influence
of this dream of a celestial glory."'
The Professor accordingly re-delivered

to Virginia the entire substance of his lectures in the ship. He fully impressed on her that all the intellect of the world was on the side of Humanity; and that God's existence could be disproved with a box of chemicals. He was agreeably surprised at finding her not at all unwilling to be convinced, and extremely unexacting in her demands for proof. In a few days she had not a remnant of superstition left. 'At last!' exclaimed the Professor; 'it has come at last. Unspeakable happiness will surely begin now.'

CHAPTER XVI.

N O one now could possibly be more emancipated than Virginia. She tittered all day long and whenever the Professor asked her why, she always told him she was thinking of 'an intelligent First Cause,' a conception which she said 'was really quite killing.' But when her first burst of intellectual excitement was over, she became more serious. 'All thought, Paul,' she said, 'is valuable mainly because it leads to action. Come, my love, my dove, my beauty, and let us kiss each other all daylong. Let us enjoy the charming license which exact thought shows us we shall never be punished for.'

This was a result of freedom that the Professor had never bargained for. He could not understand it, 'because,' he argued, 'if people were to reason in that way, morality would at once cease to be possible.' But he had seen so much of the world lately, that he soon recovered himself, and recollecting that immorality was only ignorance, he began to show Virginia where her error lay— her one remaining error. 'I perceive,' he said, 'that you are ignorant of one

of the greatest triumphs of exact thought
—the distinction it has established between the lower and the higher pleasures.
Philosophers, who have thought the whole
thing over in their studies, have become
sure that as soon as the latter are
presented to men they will at once leave
all and follow them.'

'They must be very nice pleasures,'
said Virginia, 'if they would make me
leave kissing you for the sake of them.'

'They *are* nice,' said the Professor.
'They are the pleasures of the imagination, the intellect, and the glorious apprehension of truth. Compared with
these, kissing me would be quite insipid.
Remain here for a moment, whilst I go

to fetch something, and you shall then begin to taste them.'

In a few moments Paul came back again, and found Virginia in a state of intense expectancy.

'Now—,' he exclaimed triumphantly.

'Now—,' exclaimed Virginia, with a beating heart.

The Professor put his hand in his pocket, and drew slowly forth from it an object which Virginia knew well. It reminded her of the most innocent period of her life; but she hated the very sight of it none the less. It was a Colenso's Arithmetic.

'Come,' said the Professor, 'no truths are so pure and necessary as those of mathematics ; you shall at once begin the glorious apprehension of them.'

'Oh, Paul,' cried Virginia, in an agony, 'but I really don't care for truth at all; and you know that when I broke your tin box open and read your private letters in my search for it, you were very angry with me.'

'Ah!' said Paul, holding up his finger, 'but those were not necessary truths. Truths about human action and character are not necessary truths ; therefore men of science care nothing about them, and they have no place in scientific systems of ethics. Pure truths are of a very different character; and, however much you may misunderstand your own inclinations, you can really care for nothing so much as doing a few sums. I will set you some very easy ones to begin with, and you shall do them by yourself, whilst I magnify in the next room the parasites of the missing link.'

Virginia saw that there was no help for it. She did her sums by herself the whole morning, which, as at school she had been very good at arithmetic, was not a hard task for her, and Paul magnified parasites in the next room, and prepared slides for his microscope.

When they met again, Paul began skipping and dancing, as if he had gone quite out of his senses, and every now and then between the skips he gave a sepulchral groan. Virginia asked him in astonishment what on earth was the matter with him.

'Matter!' he exclaimed. 'Why, Humanity is at last perfect! All the evils of existence are removed; we neither of us believe in a God or a celestial future; and we are both in full enjoyment of the higher pleasures and the apprehension of scientific truth. And therefore I skip because Humanity is so unspeakably happy, and I groan because it is so unspeakably solemn.'

'Alas! alas!' cried Virginia, 'and would not you like to kiss me?'

'No,' said the Professor, sternly; 'and you would not like me to kiss you. It is impossible that one half of Humanity should prefer the pleasure of unlawful love to the pleasure of finding out scientific truths.'

'But,' pleaded Virginia, 'cannot we enjoy both ?'

'No,' said the Professor, 'for if I began to kiss you I should soon not care two straws about the parasites of the missing link.'

'Well,' said Virginia, 'it is nice of you to say that; but still——Ah me! Ah me!'

And her bosom heaved slowly with a soft, long sigh.

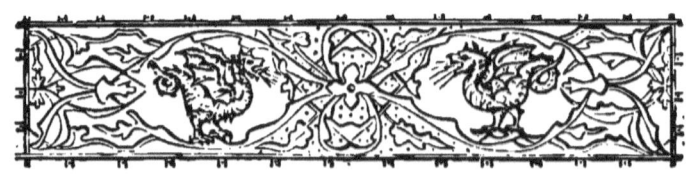

CHAPTER XVII.

IRGINIA was preparing, with a rueful face, to resume her enjoyment of the higher pleasures, when a horrible smell, like that of an open drain, was suddenly blown in through the window.

Virginia stopped her nose with her handkerchief. The Professor's conduct was very different.

'Oh, rapture!' he cried, jumping up

from his seat, 'I smell the missing link.' And in another instant he was gone.

'Well,' said Virginia, 'here is one comfort. Whilst Paul is away I shall be relieved from the higher pleasures. Alas!' she cried, as she flung herself down on the sofa, 'he is so nice-looking, and such an enlightened thinker. But it is plain he has never loved, or else very certainly he would love again.'

Paul returned in about a couple of hours, again unsuccessful in his search.

'Ah!' cried Virginia, 'I am so glad you have not caught the creature!'

'Glad!' echoed the Professor, 'glad! Do you know that till I have caught the missing link the cause of glorious truth will suffer grievously? The missing link is the token of the solemn fact of our origin from inorganic matter. I did but catch one blessed glimpse of him. He had certainly a silver band about his neck. He was about three feet high. He was rolling in a lump of carrion. It is through him that we are related to the stars—the holy, the glorious stars, about which we know so little.'

'Bother the stars!' said Virginia; 'I couldn't bear, Paul, that anything should come between you and me. I have been thinking of you and longing for you the whole time you have been away.'

'What!' cried Paul, 'and how have

you been able to forego the pleasures of the intellect ? '

' I have deserted them,' cried Virginia, 'for the pleasures of the imagination, which I gathered from you were also very ennobling. And I found they were so ; for I have been imagining that you loved me. Why is the reality less ennobling than the imagination ? Paul, you shall love me; I will force you to love me. It will make us both so happy : we shall never go to hell for it ; and it cannot possibly cause the slightest scandal.'

The Professor was more bewildered than ever by these appeals. He wondered how Humanity would ever get on if one half of it cared nothing for pure truth, and persisted in following the vulgar impulses that had been the most distinguishing feature of its benighted past—that is to say, those ages of its existence of which any record has been preserved for us.   Luckily, however, Virginia came to his assistance.

'I think I know, Paul,' she said, 'why I do not care as I should do for the intellectual pleasures.   We have both been seeking them by ourselves; and we have been therefore egoistic hedonists. It is quite true, as you say, that selfishness is a despicable thing.   Let me,' she went on, sitting down beside him, 'look through your microscope along with you.

I think perhaps, if we shared the pleasure, the missing link's parasites might have some interest for me.'

The Professor was overjoyed at this proposal. The two sat down side by side, and tried their best to look simultaneously through the eye-piece of the microscope. Virginia in a moment expressed herself much satisfied. It is true they saw nothing; but their cheeks touched. The Professor too seemed contented, and said they should both be in a state of rapture when they had got the right focus. At last Virginia whispered, with a soft smile—

'Suppose we put that nasty microscope aside; it is only in the way. And then, oh, Paul; dear love, dove of a Paul! we can kiss each other to our heart's content.'

Paul thought Virginia quite incorrigible, and rushed headlong out of the room.

CHAPTER XVIII.

' **A**LAS !' cried Paul, 'what can be done to convince one half of Humanity that it is really devoted to the higher pleasures and does not care for the lower—at least nothing to speak of?' The poor man was in a state of dreadful perplexity, and felt well-nigh distracted. At last a light broke in on him. He remembered that as one of his most revered masters, Professor Tyndall, had admitted, a great part of

Humanity would always need a religion, and that Virginia now had none. He at once rushed back to her. ' Ah !' he exclaimed, 'all is explained now. You cannot be in love with me, for that would be unlawful passion. Unlawful passion is unreasonable, and unreasonable passion would quite upset a system of pure reason, which is what exact thought shows us is soon going to govern the world. No ! the emotions that you fancy are directed to me are in reality cosmic emotion—in other words, are the reasonable religion of the future. I must now initiate you in its solemn and unspeakably significant worship.'

' Religion !' exclaimed Virginia, not

knowing whether to laugh or cry. ' It
is not kind of you to be making fun of
me. There is no God, no soul, and no
supernatural order, and above all there
is no hell. How then can you talk to
me about religion ? '

'You,' replied Paul, 'are associating
religion with theology, as indeed the
world hitherto always has done. But
those two things, as Professor Huxley
well observes, have absolutely nothing
to do with each other. " It may be,"
says that great teacher, " that the object
of a man's religion is an ideal of sensual
enjoyment, or——" '

' Ah !' cried Virginia, 'that is my religion, Paul.'

' Nonsense ! ' replied 'Paul ; 'that cannot be the religion of half Humanity,
else high, holy, solemn, awful morality
would never be able to stand on its own
basis. See, the night has fallen, the
glorious moon has arisen, the stupendous
stars are sparkling in the firmament.
Come down with me to the sea-shore,
where we may be face to face with
nature, and I will show you then what
true religion—what true worship is.'

The two went out together. They
stood on the smooth sands, which glittered
white and silvery in the dazzling moonlight. All was hushed. The gentle
murmur of the trees, and the soft splash
of the sea, seemed· only to make the

silence audible. The Professor paused close beside Virginia, and took her hand. Virginia liked that, and thought that religion without theology was not perhaps so bad after all. Meanwhile Paul had fixed his eyes on the moon. Then, in a voice almost broken with emotion, he whispered, 'The prayer of the man of science, it has been said, must be for the most part of the silent sort. He who said that was wrong. It need not be silent; it need only be inarticulate. I have discovered an audible and a reasonable liturgy which will give utterance to the full to the religion of exact thought. Let us both join our voices, and let us croon at the moon.'

The Professor at once began a long, low howling. Virginia joined him, until she was out of breath.

'Oh, Paul,' she said at last, 'is this more rational than the Lord's Prayer?'

'Yes,' said the Professor, 'for we can analyse and comprehend that; but true religious feeling, as Professor Tyndall tells us, we can neither analyse nor comprehend. See how big nature is, and how little—ah, how little!—we know about it. Is it not solemn, and sublime, and awful? Come let us howl again.'

The Professor's devotional fervour grew every moment. At last he put his hand to his mouth, and began hooting like an owl, till it seemed that all the island echoed to him. The louder Paul hooted and howled, the more near did he draw to Virginia.

'Ah!' he said, as he put his arm about her waist, 'it is in solemn moments like this that the solidarity of mankind becomes apparent.'

Virginia, during the last few moments, had stuck her fingers in her ears. She now took them out, and, throwing her arms round Paul's neck, tried, with her cheek on his shoulder, to make another little hoot; but the sound her lips formed was much more like a kiss. The power of religion was at last too much for Paul.

'For the sake of cosmic emotion,'

K

he exclaimed, 'O other half of Humanity, and for the sake of rational religion, both of which are showing themselves under quite a new light to me, I will kiss you.'

The Professor was bending down his face over her, when, as if by magic, he started, stopped, and remained as one petrified. Amidst the sharp silence, there rang a human shout from the rocks.

'Oh!' shrieked Virginia, falling on her knees, 'it is a miracle! it is a miracle! And I know—merciful heavens —I know the meaning of it. God is angry with us for pretending that we do not believe on Him.'

The Professor was as white as a sheet; but he struggled with his perturbation manfully.

'It is not a miracle,' he cried, 'but an hallucination. It is an axiom with exact thinkers that all proofs of the miraculous are hallucinations.'

'See,' shrieked Virginia again, 'they are coming, they are coming. Do not you see them?'

Paul looked, and there sure enough, were two figures, a male and a female, advancing slowly towards them, across the moonlit sand.

'It is nothing,' cried Paul; 'it cannot possibly be anything. I protest, in the name of science, that it is an optical delusion.'

Suddenly the female figure exclaimed, 'Thank God, it is he!'

In another moment the male figure exclaimed, 'Thank God, it is she!'

'My husband!' gasped Virginia.

'My wife!' replied the bishop, for it was none other than he. 'Welcome to Chasuble Island. By the blessing of God it is on your own home you have been wrecked, and you have been living in the very house that I had intended to prepare for you. Providentially, too, Professor Darnley's wife has called here, in her search for her husband, who has overstayed his time.

See, my love, my dove, my beauty, here is the monkey I promised you as a pet, which broke loose a few days ago, and which I was in the act of looking for when your joint cries attracted us, and we found you.'

A yell of delight here broke from the Professor. The eyes of the others were turned on him, and he was seen embracing wildly a monkey which the bishop led by a chain. 'The missing link!' he exclaimed, 'the missing link!'

'Nonsense!' cried the sharp tones of a lady with a green gown and grey corkscrew curls. 'It is nothing but a monkey that the good bishop has been trying to tame for his wife. Don't you see her name engraved on the collar?'

The shrill accents acted like a charm upon Paul. He sprang away from the creature that he had been just caressing. He gazed for a moment on Virginia's lovely form, her exquisite toilette, and her melting eyes. Then he turned wildly to the green gown and the grey corkscrew curls. Sorrow and superstition, he felt, were again invading Humanity. 'Alas!' he exclaimed at last, 'I do now indeed believe in hell.'

'And I,' cried Virginia, with much greater tact, and rushing into the arms of her bishop, 'once more believe in heaven.'

NOTES.

'WE now find it (*the earth*) not only swathed by an atmosphere, and covered by a sea, but also crowded with living things. The question is, how were they introduced? . . . The conclusion of science would undoubtedly be, that the molten earth contained within it elements of life, which grouped themselves into their present forms as the planet cooled. The ' difficulty and reluctance encountered by this concep-tion arise *solely* from the fact that the theologic con-ception obtained a prior footing in the human mind. . . . Were not man's origin implicated, we should accept without a murmur the derivation of animal and vegetable life from what we call inorganic nature. The conclusion of pure intellect points this way, and no other.' PROFESSOR TYNDALL.

'Is this egg (*from which the human being springs*) matter? I hold it to be so, as much as the seed of a fern or of an oak. Nine months go to the making of it into a man. Are the additions made during this period of gestation drawn from matter? I think so, undoubtedly. If there be anything besides matter in the egg, or in the infant subsequently slumbering in the womb, what is it?' PROFESSOR TYNDALL.

'Matter I define as the mysterious thing by which all this is accomplished.' PROFESSOR TYNDALL.

'I do not think that the materialist is entitled to say that his molecular groupings and motions explain everything. In reality, they *explain* nothing.'
                              PROFESSOR TYNDALL.

'Who shall exaggerate the deadly influence on personal morality of those theologies which have represented the Deity . . . as a sort of pedantic drill-sergeant of mankind, to whom no valour, no long-tried loyalty, could atone for the misplacement of a button of the uniform, or the misunderstanding of a paragraph of the "regulations and instructions"?'
                              PROFESSOR HUXLEY.

'(*To the Jesuit imagination*) God is obviously a large individual, who holds the leading-strings of the universe, and orders its steps from a position outside it all. . . . According to it (*this notion*) the Power whom Goethe does not dare to name, and whom Gassendi and Clark Maxwell present to us under the guise of a manufacturer of atoms, turns out annually, for England and Wales alone, a quarter of a million of new souls. Taken in connection with the dictum of Mr. Carlyle, that this annual increment to our population are " mostly fools," but little profit to the human heart seems derivable from this mode of re-garding the divine operations. . . . In the presence of this mystery (*the mystery of life*) the notion of an atomic manufacturer and artificer of souls, raises the doubt whether those who entertain it were ever really penetrated by the solemnity of the problem for which they offer such a solution.'

PROFESSOR TYNDALL.

' I look forward, however, to a time when the strength, insight, and elevation which now visit us in mere hints and glimpses, during moments of clear-ness and vigour, shall be the stable and permanent

possession of purer and mightier minds than ours—
purer and mightier, partly because of their deeper
knowledge of matter, and their more faithful conformity to its laws.' PROFESSOR TYNDALL.

'The world, as it is, is growing daily dimmer before my eyes. The world, as it is to be, is ever growing brighter.' HARRIET MARTINEAU.

'. . . When you and I, like streaks of morning
cloud, shall have melted into the infinite azure of the
past.' PROFESSOR TYNDALL.

'We, too, turn our thoughts to that which is behind the veil. We strive to pierce its secret with eyes,
we trust, as eager and as fearless, and even, it may
be, more patient in searching for realities behind the
gloom. That which shall come *after* is no less
solemn to us than to you.'

MR. FREDERIC HARRISON.

'Theological hypotheses of a new and hetero-
geneous existence have deadened our interest in the
realities, the grandeur, and the perpetuity of an
earthly life.' MR. FREDERIC HARRISON.

'As we read the calm and humane words of Condorcet, on the very edge of his yawning grave, we learn, from the conviction of posthumous activity (not posthumous fame), how the consciousness of a living incorporation with the glorious future of his race, can give a patience and happiness equal to that of any martyr of theology. . . . Once make it (*i.e.* "this sense of posthumous participation in the life of our fellows") the basis of philosophy, the standard of right and wrong, and the centre of a religion, and this (*the conversion of the masses*) will prove, perhaps, an easier task than that of teaching Greeks and Romans, Syrians and Moors, to look forward to a life of ceaseless psalmody in an immaterial heaven.'

MR. FREDERIC HARRISON.

'We make the future life, in the truest sense, social, inasmuch as our future is simply an active existence prolonged by society; and our future life rests not in any vague yearning, of which we have as little evidence as we have definite conception : it rests on a perfectly certain truth . . . that the actions, feelings, thoughts, of each one of us, do marvellously influence and mould each other. . . . Can we conceive a more potent stimulus to rectitude, to daily and hourly striving after a true life, than this ever-present sense that we are indeed immortal ; not that we have an immortal something within us—but that in very truth we ourselves, our thinking, feeling, acting personalities, are immortal?'

Mr. Frederic Harrison.

'As we *live for others* in life, so we *live in others* after death. . . . How deeply does such a belief as this bring home to each moment of life the mysterious perpetuity of ourselves! For good, for evil, we cannot die. We cannot shake ourselves free from this eternity of our faculties.' Mr. Frederic Harrison.

'We cannot even say that we shall continue to love ; but we know that we shall be loved.'

Mr. Frederic Harrison.

'It is only when an earthly future is the fulfilment of a worthy earthly life, that we can see the majesty, as well as the glory, of the world beyond the grave ; and then only will it fulfil its moral and religious purpose as the great guide of human conduct.'

Mr. Frederic Harrison.

'I am confident that a brighter day is coming for future generations.' HARRIET MARTINEAU.

' The humblest life that ever turned a sod sends a wave—no, more than a wave, a life—through the ever-growing harmony of human society.'

MR. FREDERIC HARRISON.

' Not a single nature, in its entirety, but leaves its influence for good or for evil. *As a fact, the good prevail.'* MR. FREDERIC HARRISON.

' To our friends and loved ones we shall give the most worthy honour and tribute if we never say nor remember that they are dead, but, contrariwise, that they have lived ; that hereby the brotherly force and flow of their action and work may be carried over the gulf of death, and made immortal in the true and healthy life which they worthily had and used.'

PROFESSOR CLIFFORD.

' It cannot be doubted that the "spiritual body" of this book (*The Unseen Universe*) will be used to support a belief that the dead are subject either to the *shame and suffering of a Christian Heaven* and Hell, or to the degrading service of a modern witch. From *each* of these *unspeakable profanities* let us hope and endeavour that the memories of great and worthy men may be finally relieved.' PROFESSOR CLIFFORD.

'I choose the noble part of Emerson, when, after various disenchantments, he exclaimed, "I covet truth." The gladness of true heroism visits the heart of him who is really competent to say this.' PROFESSOR TYNDALL.

'The highest, as it is the only, content is to be attained, not by grovelling in the rank and steaming valleys of sense, but by continually striving towards those high peaks, when, resting in eternal calm, reason discerns the undefined but bright ideal of the highest good—"a cloud by day, a pillar of fire by night."' PROFESSOR HUXLEY.

'If it can be shown by observation and experiment, that theft, murder, and adultery, do not tend to diminish the happiness of society, then, in the absence of any but natural knowledge, they are not social immoralities.' PROFESSOR HUXLEY.

'For my own part, I do not for one moment admit that morality is not strong enough to hold its own.' PROFESSOR HUXLEY.

'I object to the very general use of the terms religion and theology, as if they were synonymous, or *indeed had anything whatever to do with one another.* . . . Religion is an affair of the affections. It may be that the object of a man's religion—the ideal which he worships—is an ideal of sensual enjoyment.'
PROFESSOR HUXLEY.

'In his hour of health . . . when the pause of reflection has set in, the scientific investigator finds himself overshadowed with the same awe. It associates him with a power which gives fulness and tone to his existence, but which he can neither analyse nor comprehend.' PROFESSOR TYNDALL.

'He will see what drivellers even men of strenuous intellects may become, though exclusively dwelling and dealing with theological chimeras.'
PROFESSOR TYNDALL.

'The two kinds of cosmic emotion run together and become one. The microcosm is viewed only in relation to human action ; nature is presented to the emotions as the guide and teacher of humanity. And the microcosm is viewed only as tending to complete correspondence with the external ; human conduct is subject for reverence only in so far as it is consonant to the demiurgic law, in harmony with the teaching of divine Nature.' PROFESSOR CLIFFORD.

'The world will have religion of some kind, even though it should fly for it to the intellectual whoredom of " spiritualism." ' PROFESSOR TYNDALL.

'All positive methods of treating man, of a comprehensive kind, adopt to the full all that has ever been said about the dignity of man's moral and spiritual life. . . . I do not confine my language to the philosophy or religion of Comte ; for the same conception of man is common to many philosophies and many religions.' MR. FREDERIC HARRISON.

PRINTED BY

SPOTTISWOODE AND CO., NEW-STRFET SQUARE

LONDON

LIST OF BOOKS PUBLISHED BY

CHATTO & WINDUS

111 ST. MARTIN'S LANE, CHARING CROSS, LONDON, W.C.

About (Edmond).—The Fellah: An Egyptian Novel. Translated by
Sir RANDAL ROBERTS. Post 8vo, illustrated boards, 2s.

Adams (W. Davenport), Works by.
A Dictionary of the Drama: being a comprehensive Guide to the Plays, Playwrights, Players,
and Playhouses of the United Kingdom and America, from the Earliest Times to the Present
Day. Crown 8vo, half-bound, 12s. 6d. [*Preparing.*
Quips and Quiddities. Selected by W. DAVENPORT ADAMS. Post 8vo, cloth limp, 2s. 6d.

Agony Column (The) of 'The Times,' from 1800 to 1870. Edited
with an Introduction, by ALICE CLAY. Post 8vo, cloth limp, 2s. 6d.

Aïdé (Hamilton), Novels by. Post 8vo, illustrated boards, 2s. each.
Carr of Carrlyon. | **Confidences.**

Alden (W. L.).—A Lost Soul: Being the Confession and Defence of
Charles Lindsay. Fcap. 8vo, cloth boards, 1s. 6d.

Alexander (Mrs.), Novels by. Post 8vo, illustrated boards, 2s. each.
Maid, Wife, or Widow? | **Valerie's Fate.** | **Blind Fate.**

Crown 8vo, cloth, 3s. 6d. each; post 8vo, picture boards, 2s. each.
A Life Interest. | **Mona's Choice.** | **By Woman's Wit.**

Allen (F. M.).—Green as Grass. With a Frontispiece. Crown 8vo,
cloth, 3s. 6d.

Allen (Grant), Works by.
The Evolutionist at Large. Crown 8vo, cloth extra, 6s.
Post-Prandial Philosophy. Crown 8vo, art linen, 3s. 6d.
Moorland Idylls. Crown 8vo, cloth decorated, 6s.

Crown 8vo, cloth extra, 3s. 6d. each; post 8vo, illustrated boards, 2s. each.

Babylon. 12 Illustrations.	**The Devil's Die.**	**The Duchess of Powysland**
Strange Stories. Frontis.	**This Mortal Coil.**	**Blood Royal.**
The Beckoning Hand.	**The Tents of Shem.** Frontis.	**Ivan Greet's Masterpiece.**
For Maimie's Sake.	**The Great Taboo.**	**The Scallywag.** 24 Illusts.
Philistia.	**Dumaresq's Daughter.**	**At Market Value.**
In all Shades.	**Under Sealed Orders.**	

Dr. Palliser's Patient. Fcap. 8vo, cloth boards, 1s. 6d.

Anderson (Mary).—Othello's Occupation: A Novel. Crown 8vo,
cloth, 3s. 6d.

Antipodean (The): An Australasian Annual. Edited by A. B. PATER-
SON and G. ESSEX EVANS. Medium 8vo, with Illustrations, 1s.

Arnold (Edwin Lester), Stories by.
The Wonderful Adventures of Phra the Phœnician. Crown 8vo, cloth extra, with 12
Illustrations by H. M. PAGET. 3s. 6d.; post 8vo, illustrated boards, 2s.
The Constable of St. Nicholas. With Frontispiece by S. L. WOOD. Crown 8vo, cloth, 3s. 6d.

Artemus Ward's Works. With Portrait and Facsimile. Crown 8vo,
cloth extra, 3s. 6d.—Also a POPULAR EDITION, post 8vo, picture boards, 2s.

Ashton (John), Works by. Crown 8vo, cloth extra, 7s. 6d. each.
History of the Chap-Books of the 18th Century. With 334 Illustrations
Humour, Wit, and Satire of the Seventeenth Century. With 82 Illustrations.
English Caricature and Satire on Napoleon the First. With 115 Illustrations.
Modern Street Ballads. With 57 Illustrations.
Social Life in the Reign of Queen Anne. With 85 Illustrations. Crown 8vo, cloth, 3s. 6d.

Bacteria, Yeast Fungi, and Allied Species, A Synopsis of. By
W. B. GROVE, B.A. With 87 Illustrations. Crown 8vo, cloth extra, 3s. 6d.

Bardsley (Rev. C. Wareing, M.A.), Works by.
English Surnames : Their Sources and Significations. FIFTH EDITION, with a New Preface
Crown 8vo, cloth, 7s. 6d.
Curiosities of Puritan Nomenclature. Crown 8vo, cloth, 3s. 6d.

Baring Gould (Sabine, Author of 'John Herring,' &c.), Novels by.
Crown 8vo, cloth extra, 3s. 6d. each; post 8vo, illustrated boards, 2s. each.
Red Spider. | **Eve.**

Barr (Robert : Luke Sharp), Stories by. Cr. 8vo, cl., 3s. 6d. each.
In a Steamer Chair. With Frontispiece and Vignette by DEMAIN HAMMOND.
From Whose Bourne, &c. With 47 Illustrations by HAL HURST and others.
A Woman Intervenes. With 8 Illustrations by HAL HURST.
Revenge! With 12 Illustrations by LANCELOT SPEED and others.

Barrett (Frank), Novels by.
Post 8vo, illustrated boards, 2s. each; cloth, 2s. 6d. each.

Fettered for Life.	**A Prodigal's Progress.**
The Sin of Olga Zassoulich.	**John Ford;** and **His Helpmate.**
Between Life and Death.	**A Recoiling Vengeance.**
Folly Morrison.	**Honest Davie.**	**Lieut. Barnabas.**	**Found Guilty.**
Little Lady Linton.	**For Love and Honour.**

Crown 8vo, cloth, 3s. 6d. each; post 8vo, picture boards, 2s. each; cloth limp, 2s. 6d. each.
The Woman of the Iron Bracelets. | **The Harding Scandal.**
A Missing Witness. With 8 Illustrations by W. H. MARGETSON. Crown 8vo, cloth, 3s. 6d.
Was She Justified? Crown 8vo, cloth, gilt top, 6s.

Barrett (Joan).—Monte Carlo Stories. Fcap. 8vo, cloth, 1s. 6d.

Beaconsfield, Lord. By T. P. O'CONNOR, M.P. Cr. 8vo, cloth, 5s.

Beauchamp (Shelsley).—Grantley Grange. Post 8vo, boards, 2s.

Besant (Sir Walter) and James Rice, Novels by.
Crown 8vo, cloth extra, 3s. 6d. each; post 8vo, illustrated boards, 2s. each; cloth limp, 2s. 6d. each.

Ready-Money Mortiboy.	**By Celia's Arbour.**
My Little Girl.	**The Chaplain of the Fleet.**
With Harp and Crown.	**The Seamy Side.**
This Son of Vulcan.	**The Case of Mr. Lucraft, &c.**
The Golden Butterfly.	**'Twas in Trafalgar's Bay, &c.**
The Monks of Thelema.	**The Ten Years' Tenant, &c.**

. There is also a LIBRARY EDITION of the above Twelve Volumes, handsomely set in new type on a large crown 8vo page, and bound in cloth extra, 6s. each; and a POPULAR EDITION of **The Golden Butterfly**, medium 8vo, 6d.; cloth, 1s.

Besant (Sir Walter), Novels by.
Crown 8vo, cloth extra, 3s. 6d. each; post 8vo, illustrated boards, 2s. each; cloth limp, 2s. 6d. each.
All Sorts and Conditions of Men. With 12 Illustrations by FRED. BARNARD.
The Captains' Room, &c. With Frontispiece by E. J. WHEELER.
All in a Garden Fair. With 6 Illustrations by HARRY FURNISS.
Dorothy Forster. With Frontispiece by CHARLES GREEN.
Uncle Jack, and other Stories. | **Children of Gibeon.**
The World Went Very Well Then. With 12 Illustrations by A. FORESTIER.
Herr Paulus : His Rise, his Greatness, and his Fall. | **The Bell of St. Paul's.**
For Faith and Freedom. With Illustrations by A. FORESTIER and F. WADDY.
To Call Her Mine, &c. With 9 Illustrations by A. FORESTIER.
The Holy Rose, &c. With Frontispiece by F. BARNARD.
Armorel of Lyonesse : A Romance of To-day. With 12 Illustrations by F. BARNARD.
St. Katherine's by the Tower. With 12 Illustrations by C. GREEN.
Verbena Camellia Stephanotis, &c. With a Frontispiece by GORDON BROWNE.
The Ivory Gate. | **The Rebel Queen.**
Beyond the Dreams of Avarice. With 12 Illustrations by W. H. HYDE.
In Deacon's Orders, &c. With Frontispiece by A. FORESTIER. | **The Revolt of Man.**
Crown 8vo, cloth extra, 3s. 6d. each.
The Master Craftsman. | **The City of Refuge.** With a Frontispiece by F. S. WILSON.
All Sorts and Conditions of Men. CHEAP POPULAR EDITION. Medium 8vo, 6d; cloth, 1s.
A Fountain Sealed. With Frontispiece by H. G. BURGESS. Crown 8vo, cloth, 6s.
The Charm, and other Drawing-room Plays. By Sir WALTER BESANT and WALTER H. POLLOCK.
With 50 Illustrations by CHRIS HAMMOND and JULE GOODMAN. Crown 8vo, cloth, gilt edges, 6s.
Fifty Years Ago. With 144 Plates and Woodcuts. Crown 8vo, cloth extra, 5s.
The Eulogy of Richard Jefferies. With Portrait. Crown 8vo, cloth extra, 6s.
London. With 125 Illustrations. Demy 8vo, cloth, 7s. 6d.
Westminster. With Etched Frontispiece by F. S. WALKER, R.P.E., and 130 Illustrations by
WILLIAM PATTEN and others. Demy 8vo, cloth, 7s. 6d.
Sir Richard Whittington. With Frontispiece. Crown 8vo, art linen, 3s. 6d.
Gaspard de Coligny. With a Portrait. Crown 8vo, art linen, 3s. 6d.

Bechstein (Ludwig).—As Pretty as Seven, and other German
Stories. With Additional Tales by the Brothers GRIMM, and 98 Illustrations by RICHTER. Square
8vo, cloth extra, 6s. 6d.; gilt edges, 7s. 6d.

Bellew (Frank).—The Art of Amusing: A Collection of Graceful
Arts, Games, Tricks, Puzzles, and Charades. With 300 Illustrations. Crown 8vo, cloth extra, 4s. 6d.

Bennett (W. C., LL.D.).—Songs for Sailors. Post 8vo, cl. limp, 2s.

Bewick (Thomas) and his Pupils. By AUSTIN DOBSON. With 95
Illustrations. Square 8vo, cloth extra, 6s.

Bierce (Ambrose).—In the Midst of Life: Tales of Soldiers and
Civilians. Crown 8vo, cloth extra, 3s. 6d.; post 8vo, illustrated boards, 2s.

Bill Nye's History of the United States. With 146 Illustrations
by F. OPPER. Crown 8vo, cloth extra, 3s. 6d.

Biré (Edmond). — Diary of a Citizen of Paris during 'The
Terror.' Translated and Edited by JOHN DE VILLIERS. With 2 Photogravure Portraits. Two Vols.
demy 8vo, cloth, 21s.

Blackburn's (Henry) Art Handbooks.

Academy Notes, 1898. [May.	**Grosvenor Notes,** Vol. III., **1888-90.** With
Academy Notes, 1875-79. Complete in	230 Illustrations. Demy 8vo cloth, 3s. 6d.
One Vol., with 600 Illustrations. Cloth, 6s.	**The New Gallery, 1888-1892.** With 250
Academy Notes, 1880-84. Complete in	Illustrations. Demy 8vo, cloth, 6s.
One Vol., with 700 Illustrations. Cloth, 6s.	**English Pictures at the National Gallery.**
Academy Notes, 1890-94. Complete in	With 114 Illustrations. 1s.
One Vol., with 800 Illustrations. Cloth, 7s. 6d.	**Old Masters at the National Gallery.**
Grosvenor Notes, Vol. I., **1877-82.** With	With 128 Illustrations. 1s. 6d.
300 Illustrations. Demy 8vo, cloth 6s.	**Illustrated Catalogue to the National**
Grosvenor Notes, Vol. II., **1883-87.** With	**Gallery.** With 242 Illusts. Demy 8vo, cloth, 3s.
300 Illustrations. Demy 8vo, cloth, 6s.	

The Illustrated Catalogue of the Paris Salon, 1898. With 300 Sketches. 3s.   [May

Blind (Mathilde), Poems by.
The Ascent of Man. Crown 8vo, cloth, 5s.
Dramas in Miniature. With a Frontispiece by F. MADOX BROWN. Crown 8vo, cloth, 5s.
Songs and Sonnets. Fcap. 8vo vellum and gold, 5s.
Birds of Passage: Songs of the Orient and Occident. Second Edition. Crown 8vo, linen, 6s. net.

Bourget (Paul).—A Living Lie. Translated by JOHN DE VILLIERS.
With special Preface for the English Edition. Crown 8vo, cloth, 3s. 6d.

Bourne (H. R. Fox), Books by.
English Merchants: Memoirs in Illustration of the Progress of British Commerce. With numerous
Illustrations. Crown 8vo, cloth extra, 7s. 6d.
English Newspapers: Chapters in the History of Journalism. Two Vols., demy 8vo, cloth, 25s.
The Other Side of the Emin Pasha Relief Expedition. Crown 8vo, cloth, 6s.

Boyle (Frederick), Works by. Post 8vo, illustrated bds., 2s. each.
Chronicles of No-Man's Land. | Camp Notes. | Savage Life.

Brand (John).—Observations on Popular Antiquities; chiefly
illustrating the Origin of our Vulgar Customs, Ceremonies, and Superstitions. With the Additions of Sir
HENRY ELLIS, and numerous Illustrations. Crown 8vo, cloth extra, 7s. 6d.

Brewer (Rev. Dr.), Works by.
The Reader's Handbook of Allusions, References, Plots, and Stories. Eighteenth
Thousand. Crown 8vo, cloth extra, 7s. 6d.
Authors and their Works, with the Dates: Being the Appendices to 'The Reader's Hand-
book,' separately printed. Crown 8vo, cloth limp, 2s.
A Dictionary of Miracles: Imitative, Realistic, and Dogmatic. Crown 8vo, cloth, 3s. 6d.

Brewster (Sir David), Works by. Post 8vo, cloth, 4s. 6d. each.
More Worlds than One: Creed of the Philosopher and Hope of the Christian. With Plates.
The Martyrs of Science: GALILEO, TYCHO BRAHE, and KEPLER. With Portraits.
Letters on Natural Magic. With numerous Illustrations.

Brillat-Savarin.— Gastronomy as a Fine Art. Translated by
R. E. ANDERSON, M.A. Post 8vo, half-bound, 2s.

Brydges (Harold).—Uncle Sam at Home. With 91 Illustrations.
Post 8vo, illustrated boards, 2s.; cloth limp, 2s. 6d.

Buchanan (Robert), Novels, &c., by.

Crown 8vo, cloth extra, 3s. 6d. each; post 8vo, illustrated boards, 2s. each.

The Shadow of the Sword.	Love Me for Ever. With Frontispiece.
A Child of Nature. With Frontispiece.	Annan Water.	Foxglove Manof.
God and the Man. With 11 Illustrations by	The New Abelard.	Rachel Dene.
Lady Kilpatrick. [FRED. BARNARD.	Matt: A Story of a Caravan. With Frontispiece.
The Martyrdom of Madeline. With	The Master of the Mine. With Frontispiece.
Frontispiece by A. W. COOPER.	The Heir of Linne.	Woman and the Man.

Red and White Heather. Crown 8vo, cloth extra, 3s. 6d.

The Wandering Jew: a Christmas Carol. Crown 8vo, cloth, 6s.

The Charlatan. By ROBERT BUCHANAN and HENRY MURRAY. Crown 8vo, cloth, with a Frontispiece by T. H. ROBINSON, 3s. 6d.; post 8vo, picture boards, 2s.

Burton (Robert).—The Anatomy of Melancholy. With Transla-
tions of the Quotations. Demy 8vo, cloth extra, 7s. 6d.
Melancholy Anatomised: An Abridgment of BURTON'S ANATOMY. Post 8vo, half-bd., 2s. 6d.

Caine (Hall), Novels by. Crown 8vo, cloth extra, 3s. 6d. each.; post
8vo, illustrated boards, 2s. each; cloth limp, 2s. 6d. each.
The Shadow of a Crime. | A Son of Hagar. | The Deemster.
Also LIBRARY EDITIONS of The Deemster and The Shadow of a Crime, set in new type,
crown 8vo, and bound uniform with The Christian, 6s. each; and the CHEAP POPULAR EDITION of
The Deemster, medium 8vo, portrait-cover, 6d.; cloth, 1s.

Cameron (Commander V. Lovett).—The Cruise of the 'Black
Prince' Privateer. Post 8vo, picture boards, 2s.

Captain Coignet, Soldier of the Empire: An Autobiography.
Edited by LOREDAN LARCHEY. Translated by Mrs. CAREY. With 100 Illustrations. Crown 8vo,
cloth, 3s. 6d.

Carlyle (Jane Welsh), Life of. By Mrs. ALEXANDER IRELAND. With
Portrait and Facsimile Letter. Small demy 8vo, cloth extra, 7s. 6d.

Carlyle (Thomas).—On the Choice of Books. Post 8vo, cl., 1s. 6d.
Correspondence of Thomas Carlyle and R. W. Emerson, 1834-1872. Edited by
C. E. NORTON. With Portraits. Two Vols., crown 8vo, cloth, 24s.

Carruth (Hayden).—The Adventures of Jones. With 17 Illustra-
tions. Fcap. 8vo, cloth, 2s.

Chambers (Robert W.), Stories of Paris Life by. Long fcap. 8vo,
cloth, 2s. 6d. each.
The King in Yellow. | In the Quarter.

Chapman's (George), Works. Vol. I., Plays Complete, including the
Doubtful Ones.—Vol. II., Poems and Minor Translations, with Essay by A. C. SWINBURNE.—Vol.
III., Translations of the Iliad and Odyssey. Three Vols., crown 8vo, cloth, 3s. 6d. each.

Chapple (J. Mitchell).—The Minor Chord: The Story of a Prima
Donna. Crown 8vo, cloth, 3s. 6d.

Chatto (W. A.) and J. Jackson.—A Treatise on Wood Engraving,
Historical and Practical. With Chapter by H. G. BOHN, and 450 fine Illusts. Large 4to, half-leather, 28s.

Chaucer for Children: A Golden Key. By Mrs. H. R. HAWEIS. With
8 Coloured Plates and 30 Woodcuts. Crown 4to, cloth extra, 3s. 6d.
Chaucer for Schools. By Mrs. H. R. HAWEIS. Demy 8vo, cloth limp, 2s. 6d.

Chess, The Laws and Practice of. With an Analysis of the Open-
ings. By HOWARD STAUNTON. Edited by R. B. WORMALD. Crown 8vo, cloth, 5s.
The Minor Tactics of Chess: A Treatise on the Deployment of the Forces in obedience to Stra-
tegic Principle. By F. K. YOUNG and E. C. HOWELL. Long fcap. 8vo, cloth, 2s. 6d.
The Hastings Chess Tournament. Containing the Authorised Account of the 230 Games
played Aug.-Sept., 1895. With Annotations by PILLSBURY, LASKER, TARRASCH, STEINITZ,
SCHIFFERS, TEICHMANN, BARDELEBEN, BLACKBURNE, GUNSBERG, TINSLEY, MASON, and
ALBIN; Biographical Sketches of the Chess Masters, and 22 Portraits. Edited by H. F. CHESHIRE.
Crown 8vo, cloth, 7s. 6d.

Clare (Austin), Stories by.
For the Love of a Lass. Post 8vo, illustrated boards, 2s.; cloth, 2s. 6d.
By the Rise of the River: Tales and Sketches in South Tynedale. Crown 8vo, buckram, gilt
top, 6s,

Clive (Mrs. Archer), Novels by. Post 8vo, illust. boards, 2s. each.
Paul Ferroll. | Why Paul Ferroll Killed his Wife.

Clodd (Edward, F.R.A.S.).—Myths and Dreams. Cr. 8vo, 3s. 6d.

Coates (Anne).—Rie's Diary. Crown 8vo, cloth, 3s. 6d.

Cobban (J. Maclaren), Novels by.
The Cure of Souls. Post 8vo, Illustrated boards, 2s.
The Red Sultan. Crown 8vo, cloth extra, 3s. 6d. ; post 8vo, illustrated boards, 2s.
The Burden of Isabel. Crown 8vo, cloth extra, 3s. 6d.

Coleman (John).—Curly: An Actor's Story. With 21 Illustrations
by J. C. DOLLMAN. Crown 8vo, picture cover, 1s.

Coleridge (M. E.).—The Seven Sleepers of Ephesus. Cloth, 1s. 6d.

Collins (C. Allston).—The Bar Sinister. Post 8vo, boards, 2s.

Collins (John Churton, M.A.), Books by.
Illustrations of Tennyson. Crown 8vo, cloth extra, 6s.
Jonathan Swift A Biographical and Critical Study. Crown 8vo, cloth extra, 8s.

Collins (Mortimer and Frances), Novels by.
Crown 8vo, cloth extra, 3s. 6d. each; post 8vo, illustrated boards, 2s. each.
From Midnight to Midnight. | Blacksmith and Scholar.
Transmigration. | You Play me False. | The Village Comedy.

Post 8vo, illustrated boards, 2s. each.
Sweet Anne Page. | A Fight with Fortune. | Sweet and Twenty. | Frances.

Collins (Wilkie), Novels by.
Crown 8vo, cloth extra, many Illustrated, 3s. 6d. each ; post 8vo, picture boards, 2s. each ;
cloth limp, 2s. 6d. each.

Antonina.	My Miscellanies.	Jezebel's Daughter.
Basil.	Armadale.	The Black Robe.
Hide and Seek.	Poor Miss Finch.	Heart and Science.
The Woman in White.	Miss or Mrs.?	'I Say No.'
The Moonstone.	The New Magdalen.	A Rogue's Life.
Man and Wife.	The Frozen Deep.	The Evil Genius.
After Dark.	The Law and the Lady.	Little Novels.
The Dead Secret.	The Two Destinies.	The Legacy of Cain.
The Queen of Hearts.	The Haunted Hotel.	Blind Love.
No Name.	The Fallen Leaves.	

POPULAR EDITIONS. Medium 8vo, 6d. each; cloth, 1s. each
The Woman in White. | The Moonstone. | Antonina.

The Woman in White and The Moonstone in One Volume, medium 8vo, cloth, 2s.

Colman's (George) Humorous Works: ' Broad Grins,' 'My Night-
gown and Slippers,' &c. With Life and Frontispiece. Crown 8vo, cloth extra, 3s. 6d.

Colquhoun (M. J.).—Every Inch a Soldier. Post 8vo, boards, 2s.

Colt-breaking, Hints on. By W. M. HUTCHISON. Cr. 8vo, cl., 3s. 6d.

Convalescent Cookery. By CATHERINE RYAN. Cr. 8vo, 1s. ; cl., 1s. 6d.

Conway (Moncure D.), Works by.
Demonology and Devil-Lore. With 65 Illustrations. Two Vols., demy 8vo, cloth, 28s.
George Washington's Rules of Civility. Fcap. 8vo, Japanese vellum, 2s. 6d.

Cook (Dutton), Novels by.
Post 8vo, illustrated boards, 2s. each.
Leo. | Paul Foster's Daughter.

Cooper (Edward H.).—Geoffory Hamilton. Cr. 8vo, cloth, 3s 6d.

Cornwall.—Popular Romances of the West of England; or, The
Drolls, Traditions, and Superstitions of Old Cornwall. Collected by ROBERT HUNT, F.R.S. With
two Steel Plates by GEORGE CRUIKSHANK. Crown 8vo, cloth, 7s. 6d.

Cotes (V. Cecil).—Two Girls on a Barge. With 44 Illustrations by
F. H. TOWNSEND. Post 8vo, cloth, 2s. 6d.

Craddock (C. Egbert), Stories by.
The Prophet of the Great Smoky Mountains. Post 8vo, Illustrated boards, 2s.
His Vanished Star. Crown 8vo, cloth extra, 3s. 6d.

Cram (Ralph Adams).—Black Spirits and White. Fcap. 8vo,
cloth 1s. 6d.

Crellin (H. N.), Books by.
Romances of the Old Seraglio. With 28 Illustrations by S. L. WOOD. Crown 8vo, cloth, 3s. 6d.
Tales of the Caliph. Crown 8vo, cloth, 2s.
The Nazarenes: A Drama. Crown 8vo, 1s.

Crim (Matt.).—Adventures of a Fair Rebel. Crown 8vo, cloth
extra, with a Frontispiece by DAN. BEARD. 3s. 6d.; post 8vo, illustrated boards, 2s.

Crockett (S. R.) and others. — Tales of Our Coast. By S. R.
CROCKETT, GILBERT PARKER, HAROLD FREDERIC, 'Q.,' and W CLARK RUSSELL. With 2
Illustrations by FRANK BRANGWYN. Crown 8vo, cloth, 3s. 6d.

Croker (Mrs. B. M.), Novels by. Crown 8vo, cloth extra, 3s. 6d.
each; post 8vo, illustrated boards, 2s. each; cloth limp, 2s. 6d. each.

Pretty Miss Neville.	Diana Barrington.	A Family Likeness.
A Bird of Passage.	Proper Pride.	'To Let.'
Village Tales and Jungle Tragedies.	Two Masters.	Mr. Jervis.
Married or Single ?	The Real Lady Hilda.	

Crown 8vo, cloth extra, 3s. 6d. each.

In the Kingdom of Kerry.	Interference.	A Third Person.

Beyond the Pale. Crown 8vo, buckram, 6s.
Miss Balmaine's Past. Crown 8vo, buckram, gilt top, 6s.

Cruikshank's Comic Almanack. Complete in Two SERIES: The
FIRST, from 1835 to 1843; the SECOND, from 1844 to 1853. A Gathering of the Best Humour of
THACKERAY, HOOD, MAYHEW, ALBERT SMITH, A'BECKETT, ROBERT BROUGH, &c. With
numerous Steel Engravings and Woodcuts by GEORGE CRUIKSHANK, HINE, LANDELLS, &c.
Two Vols., crown 8vo, cloth gilt, 7s. 6d. each.
The Life of George Cruikshank. By BLANCHARD JERROLD. With 84 Illustrations and a
Bibliography. Crown 8vo, cloth extra, 3s. 6d.

Cumming (C. F. Gordon), Works by. Demy 8vo, cl. ex., 8s. 6d. ea.
In the Hebrides. With an Autotype Frontispiece and 23 Illustrations.
In the Himalayas and on the Indian Plains. With 42 Illustrations.
Two Happy Years in Ceylon. With 28 Illustrations.

Via Cornwall to Egypt. With a Photogravure Frontispiece. Demy 8vo, cloth, 7s. 6d.

Cussans (John E.).—A Handbook of Heraldry; with Instructions
for Tracing Pedigrees and Deciphering Ancient MSS., &c. Fourth Edition, revised, with 408 Woodcuts
and 2 Coloured Plates. Crown 8vo, cloth extra, 6s.

Cyples (W.).—Hearts of Gold. Cr. 8vo, cl., 3s. 6d.; post 8vo, bds., 2s.

Daudet (Alphonse).—The Evangelist; or, Port Salvation. Crown
8vo, cloth extra, 3s. 6d.; post 8vo, illustrated boards, 2s.

Davenant (Francis, M.A.).—Hints for Parents on the Choice of
a Profession for their Sons when Starting in Life. Crown 8vo, cloth, 1s. 6d.

Davidson (Hugh Coleman).—Mr. Sadler's Daughters. With a
Frontispiece by STANLEY WOOD. Crown 8vo, cloth extra, 3s. 6d.

Davies (Dr. N. E. Yorke-), Works by. Cr. 8vo, 1s. ea.; cl., 1s. 6d. ea.
One Thousand Medical Maxims and Surgical Hints.
Nursery Hints : A Mother's Guide in Health and Disease.
Foods for the Fat : A Treatise on Corpulency, and a Dietary for Its Cure.

Aids to Long Life. Crown 8vo, 2s.; cloth limp, 2s. 6d.

Davies' (Sir John) Complete Poetical Works. Collected and Edited,
with Introduction and Notes, by Rev. A. B. GROSART, D.D. Two Vols., crown 8vo, cloth, 3s. 6d. each.

Dawson (Erasmus, M.B.).—The Fountain of Youth. Crown 8vo,
cloth extra, with Two Illustrations by HUME NISBET, 3s. 6d.; post 8vo, illustrated boards, 2s.

De Guerin (Maurice), The Journal of. Edited by G. S. TREBUTIEN.
With a Memoir by SAINTE-BEUVE. Translated from the 20th French Edition by JESSIE P. FROTH-
INGHAM. Fcap. 8vo, half-bound, 2s. 6d.

De Maistre (Xavier).—A Journey Round my Room. Translated
by Sir HENRY ATTWELL. Post 8vo, cloth limp, 2s. 6d.

De Mille (James).—A Castle in Spain. Crown 8vo, cloth extra, with
a Frontispiece, 3s. 6d.; post 8vo, illustrated boards, 2s.

Derby (The) : The Blue Ribbon of the Turf. With Brief Accounts
of THE OAKS, By LOUIS HENRY CURZON. Crown 8vo, cloth limp, 2s. 6d.

Derwent (Leith), Novels by. Cr. 8vo, cl., 3s. 6d. ea. ; post 8vo, 2s. ea.
Our Lady of Tears. | Circe's Lovers.

Dewar (T. R.).—A Ramble Round the Globe. With 220 Illustrations. Crown 8vo, cloth extra, 7s. 6d.

De Windt (Harry).—Through the Gold-Fields of Alaska to Bering Straits. With Map and 33 full-page Illustrations. Demy 8vo, cloth extra. 16s.

Dickens (Charles).—About England with Dickens. By ALFRED RIMMER. With 57 Illustrations by C. A. VANDERHOOF, ALFRED RIMMER, and others. Square 8vo, cloth extra, 7s. 6d.

Dictionaries.
The Reader's Handbook of Allusions, References, Plots, and Stories. By the Rev. E. C. BREWER, LL.D. With an ENGLISH BIBLIOGRAPHY. Crown 8vo, cloth extra, 7s. 6d.
Authors and their Works, with the Dates. Crown 8vo, cloth limp, 2s.
A Dictionary of Miracles: Imitative, Realistic, and Dogmatic. By the Rev. E. C. BREWER, LL.D. Crown 8vo, cloth, 3s. 6d.
Familiar Short Sayings of Great Men. With Historical and Explanatory Notes by SAMUEL A. BENT, A.M. Crown 8vo, cloth extra, 7s. 6d.
The Slang Dictionary: Etymological, Historical, and Anecdotal. Crown 8vo, cloth, 6s. 6d.
Words, Facts, and Phrases: A Dictionary of Curious, Quaint, and Out-of-the-Way Matters. By ELIEZER EDWARDS. Crown 8vo, cloth extra, 3s. 6d.

Diderot.—The Paradox of Acting. Translated, with Notes, by WALTER HERRIES POLLOCK. With Preface by Sir HENRY IRVING. Crown 8vo, parchment, 4s. 6d.

Dobson (Austin), Works by.
Thomas Bewick and his Pupils. With 95 Illustrations. Square 8vo, cloth, 6s.
Four Frenchwomen. With Four Portraits. Crown 8vo, buckram, gilt top, 6s.
Eighteenth Century Vignettes. IN THREE SERIES. Crown 8vo, buckram, 6s. each.

Dobson (W. T.).—Poetical Ingenuities and Eccentricities. Post 8vo, cloth limp, 2s. 6d.

Donovan (Dick), Detective Stories by.
Post 8vo, illustrated boards, 2s. each ; cloth limp, 2s. 6d. each.
The Man-Hunter. | Wanted !
Caught at Last.
Tracked and Taken.
Who Poisoned Hetty Duncan?
Suspicion Aroused.

A Detective's Triumphs.
In the Grip of the Law.
From Information Received.
Link by Link. | Dark Deeds.
Riddles Read.

Crown 8vo, cloth extra, 3s. 6d. each ; post 8vo, illustrated boards, 2s. each ; cloth, 2s. 6d. each.
The Man from Manchester. With 23 Illustrations.
Tracked to Doom. With Six full-page Illustrations by GORDON BROWNE.
The Mystery of Jamaica Terrace.
The Chronicles of Michael Danevitch, of the Russian Secret Service.

Dowling (Richard).—Old Corcoran's Money. Crown 8vo, cl., 3s. 6d.

Doyle (A. Conan).—The Firm of Girdlestone. Cr. 8vo, cl., 3s. 6d.

Dramatists, The Old. Cr. 8vo, cl. ex., with Portraits, 3s. 6d. per Vol.
Ben Jonson's Works. With Notes, Critical and Explanatory, and a Biographical Memoir by WILLIAM GIFFORD. Edited by Colonel CUNNINGHAM. Three Vols.
Chapman's Works. Three Vols. Vol. I. contains the Plays complete ; Vol. II., Poems and Minor Translations, with an Essay by A. C. SWINBURNE ; Vol. III., Translations of the Iliad and Odyssey.
Marlowe's Works. Edited, with Notes, by Colonel CUNNINGHAM. One Vol.
Massinger's Plays. From GIFFORD'S Text. Edited by Colonel CUNNINGHAM. One Vol.

Duncan (Sara Jeannette: Mrs. EVERARD COTES), Works by.
Crown 8vo, cloth extra, 7s. 6d. each.
A Social Departure. With 111 Illustrations by F. H. TOWNSEND.
An American Girl in London. With 80 Illustrations by F. H. TOWNSEND.
The Simple Adventures of a Memsahib. With 37 Illustrations by F. H. TOWNSEND.

Crown 8vo, cloth extra, 3s. 6d. each.
A Daughter of To-Day. | Vernon's Aunt. With 47 Illustrations by HAL HURST.

Dutt (Romesh C.).—England and India: A Record of Progress during One Hundred Years. Crown 8vo, cloth, 2s.

Dyer (T. F. Thiselton).—The Folk-Lore of Plants. Cr. 8vo, cl., 6s.

Early English Poets. Edited, with Introductions and Annotations by Rev. A. B. GROSART, D.D. Crown 8vo, cloth boards, 3s. 6d. per Volume.
Fletcher's (Giles) Complete Poems. One Vol.
Davies' (Sir John) Complete Poetical Works. Two Vols.
Herrick's (Robert) Complete Collected Poems. Three Vols.
Sidney's (Sir Philip) Complete Poetical Works. Three Vols.

Edgcumbe (Sir E. R. Pearce).—Zephyrus: A Holiday in Brazil and on the River Plate. With 41 Illustrations. Crown 8vo, cloth extra, 5s.

Edwardes (Mrs. Annie), Novels by.
Post 8vo, illustrated boards, 2s. each.
Archie Lovell. | **A Point of Honour.**

Edwards (Eliezer).—Words, Facts, and Phrases: A Dictionary
of Curious, Quaint, and Out-of-the-Way Matters. Cheaper Edition. Crown 8vo, cloth, 3s. 6d.

Edwards (M. Betham-), Novels by.
Kitty. Post 8vo, boards, 2s. ; cloth, 2s. 6d. | **Felicia.** Post 8vo, illustrated boards, 2s.

Egerton (Rev. J. C., M.A.).—Sussex Folk and Sussex Ways.
With Introduction by Rev. Dr. H. WACE, and Four Illustrations. Crown 8vo, cloth extra, 5s.

Eggleston (Edward).—Roxy: A Novel. Post 8vo, illust. boards, 2s.

Englishman's House, The: A Practical Guide for Selecting or Building a House. By C. J. RICHARDSON. Coloured Frontispiece and 534 Illusts. Cr. 8vo, cloth, 3s. 6d.

Ewald (Alex. Charles, F.S.A.), Works by.
The Life and Times of Prince Charles Stuart, Count of Albany (THE YOUNG PRETENDER). With a Portrait. Crown 8vo, cloth extra, 7s. 6d.
Stories from the State Papers. With Autotype Frontispiece. Crown 8vo, cloth, 6s.

Eyes, Our: How to Preserve Them. By JOHN BROWNING. Cr. 8vo, 1s.

Familiar Short Sayings of Great Men. By SAMUEL ARTHUR BENT,
A.M. Fifth Edition, Revised and Enlarged. Crown 8vo, cloth extra, 7s. 6d.

Faraday (Michael), Works by. Post 8vo, cloth extra, 4s. 6d. each.
The Chemical History of a Candle: Lectures delivered before a Juvenile Audience. Edited by WILLIAM CROOKES, F.C.S. With numerous Illustrations.
On the Various Forces of Nature, and their Relations to each other. Edited by WILLIAM CROOKES, F.C.S. With Illustrations.

Farrer (J. Anson), Works by.
Military Manners and Customs. Crown 8vo, cloth extra, 6s.
War: Three Essays, reprinted from 'Military Manners and Customs.' Crown 8vo, 1s. ; cloth, 1s. 6d.

Fenn (G. Manville), Novels by.
Crown 8vo, cloth extra, 3s. 6d. each ; post 8vo, illustrated boards, 2s. each.
The New Mistress. | **Witness to the Deed.** | **The Tiger Lily.** | **The White Virgin.**
A Woman Worth Winning. Crown 8vo, cloth, gilt top, 6s.

Fin-Bec.—The Cupboard Papers: Observations on the Art of Living
and Dining. Post 8vo, cloth limp, 2s. 6d.

Fireworks, The Complete Art of Making; or, The Pyrotechnist's
Treasury. By THOMAS KENTISH. With 267 Illustrations. Crown 8vo, cloth, 5s.

First Book, My. By WALTER BESANT, JAMES PAYN, W. CLARK RUS-
SELL, GRANT ALLEN, HALL CAINE, GEORGE R. SIMS, RUDYARD KIPLING, A. CONAN DOYLE,
M. E. BRADDON, F. W. ROBINSON, H. RIDER HAGGARD, R. M. BALLANTYNE, I. ZANGWILL,
MORLEY ROBERTS, D. CHRISTIE MURRAY, MARY CORELLI, J. K. JEROME, JOHN STRANGE
WINTER, BRET HARTE, 'Q.,' ROBERT BUCHANAN, and R. L. STEVENSON. With a Prefatory Story
by JEROME K. JEROME, and 185 Illustrations. A New Edition. Small demy 8vo, art linen, 3s. 6d.

Fitzgerald (Percy), Works by.
Little Essays: Passages from the Letters of CHARLES LAMB. Post 8vo, cloth, 2s. 6d.
Fatal Zero. Crown 8vo, cloth extra, 3s. 6d. ; post 8vo, illustrated boards, 2s.

Post 8vo, illustrated boards, 2s. each.

Bella Donna.	**The Lady of Brantome.**	**The Second Mrs. Tillotson.**
Polly.	**Never Forgotten.**	**Seventy-five Brooke Street.**

The Life of James Boswell (of Auchinleck). With Illusts. Two Vols., demy 8vo, cloth, 24s.
The Savoy Opera. With 60 Illustrations and Portraits. Crown 8vo, cloth, 3s. 6d.
Sir Henry Irving: Twenty Years at the Lyceum. With Portrait. Crown 8vo, 1s. ; cloth, 1s. 6d.

Flammarion (Camille), Works by.
Popular Astronomy: A General Description of the Heavens. Translated by J. ELLARD GORE,
F.R.A.S. With Three Plates and 283 Illustrations. Medium 8vo, cloth, 10s. 6d.
Urania: A Romance. With 87 Illustrations. Crown 8vo, cloth extra, 5s.

Fletcher's (Giles, B.D.) Complete Poems: Christ's Victorie in
Heaven, Christ's Victorie on Earth, Christ's Triumph over Death, and Minor Poems. With Notes by
Rev. A. B. GROSART, D.D. Crown 8vo, cloth boards, 3s. 6d.

Fonblanque (Albany) —Filthy Lucre. Post 8vo, illust. boards, 2s.

Forbes (Archibald).—The Life of Napoleon III. With Photo-
gravure Frontispiece and Thirty-six full-page Illustrations. Demy 8vo, cloth, gilt top, 12s.

Fowler (J. Kersley).—Records of Old Times: Historical, Social,
Political, Sporting, and Agricultural. With Eight full-page Illustrations. Demy 8vo, cloth, 10s. 6d.

Francillon (R. E.), Novels by.
Crown 8vo, cloth extra, 3s. 6d. each; post 8vo, illustrated boards, 2s. each.
One by One. | A Real Queen. | A Dog and his Shadow.
Ropes of Sand. Illustrated

Post 8vo, illustrated boards, 2s. each.
Queen Cophetua. | Olympia. | Romances of the Law. | King or Knave?
Jack Doyle's Daughter. Crown 8vo, cloth, 3s. 6d.

Frederic (Harold), Novels by. Post 8vo, cloth extra, 3s. 6d. each;
illustrated boards, 2s. each.
Seth's Brother's Wife. | The Lawton Girl.

French Literature, A History of. By HENRY VAN LAUN. Three
Vols., demy 8vo, cloth boards, 7s. 6d. each.

Fry's (Herbert) Royal Guide to the London Charities. Edited
by JOHN LANE. Published Annually. Crown 8vo, cloth, 1s. 6d.

Gardening Books. Post 8vo, 1s. each; cloth limp. 1s. 6d. each.
A Year's Work in Garden and Greenhouse. By GEORGE GLENNY.
Household Horticulture. By TOM and JANE JERROLD. Illustrated.
The Garden that Paid the Rent. By TOM JERROLD.
My Garden Wild. By FRANCIS G. HEATH. Crown 8vo, cloth, gilt edges, 6s.

Gardner (Mrs. Alan).—Rifle and Spear with the Rajpoots: Being
the Narrative of a Winter's Travel and Sport in Northern India. With numerous Illustrations by the
Author and F. H. TOWNSEND. Demy 4to, half-bound, 21s.

Garrett (Edward).—The Capel Girls: A Novel. Post 8vo, illustrated
boards, 2s.

Gaulot (Paul).—The Red Shirts: A Story of the Revolution. Translated by JOHN DE VILLIERS. With a Frontispiece by STANLEY WOOD. Crown 8vo, cloth, 3s. 6d.

Gentleman's Magazine, The. 1s. Monthly. Contains Stories,
Articles upon Literature, Science, Biography, and Art, and 'Table Talk' by SYLVANUS URBAN.
⁎ Bound Volumes for recent years kept in stock, 8s. 6d. each. Cases for binding, 2s. each.

Gentleman's Annual, The. Published Annually in November. 1s.

German Popular Stories. Collected by the Brothers GRIMM and
Translated by EDGAR TAYLOR. With Introduction by JOHN RUSKIN, and 22 Steel Plates after
GEORGE CRUIKSHANK. Square 8vo, cloth, 6s. 6d.; gilt edges, 7s. 6 f.

Gibbon (Chas.), Novels by. Cr. 8vo, cl., 3s. 6d. ea.; post 8vo, bds., 2s. ea.
Robin Gray. With Frontispiece. | Loving a Dream.
The Golden Shaft. With Frontispiece. | Of High Degree.

Post 8vo, illustrated boards, 2s. each.
The Flower of the Forest. | In Love and War.
The Dead Heart. | A Heart's Problem.
For Lack of Gold. | By Mead and Stream.
What Will the World Say? | The Braes of Yarrow.
For the King. | A Hard Knot. | Fancy Free.
Queen of the Meadow. | In Honour Bound.
In Pastures Green. | Heart's Delight. | Blood-Money.

Gibney (Somerville).—Sentenced! Crown 8vo, cloth, 1s. 6d.

Gilbert (W. S.), Original Plays by. In Three Series, 2s. 6d. each.
The FIRST SERIES contains: The Wicked World—Pygmalion and Galatea—Charity—The Princess—
The Palace of Truth—Trial by Jury.
The SECOND SERIES: Broken Hearts—Engaged—Sweethearts—Gretchen—Dan Druce—Tom Cobb
—H.M.S. 'Pinafore'—The Sorcerer—The Pirates of Penzance.
The THIRD SERIES: Comedy and Tragedy—Foggerty's Fairy—Rosencrantz and Guildenstern—
Patience—Princess Ida—The Mikado—Ruddigore—The Yeomen of the Guard—The Gondoliers—
The Mountebanks—Utopia.

Eight Original Comic Operas written by W. S. GILBERT. In Two Series. Demy 8vo, cloth,
2s. 6d. each. The FIRST containing: The Sorcerer—H.M.S. 'Pinafore'—The Pirates of Penzance—
Iolanthe—Patience—Princess Ida—The Mikado—Trial by Jury.
The SECOND SERIES containing: The Gondoliers—The Grand Duke—The Yeomen of the Guard—
His Excellency—Utopia, Limited—Ruddigore—The Mountebanks—Haste to the Wedding.
The Gilbert and Sullivan Birthday Book: Quotations for Every Day in the Year, selected
from Plays by W. S. GILBERT set to Music by Sir A. SULLIVAN. Compiled by ALEX. WATSON.
Royal 16mo, Japanese leather, 2s. 6d.

Gilbert (William), Novels by. Post 8vo, illustrated bds., 2s. each.
Dr. Austin's Guests. | James Duke, Costermonger.
The Wizard of the Mountain.

Glanville (Ernest), Novels by.
Crown 8vo, cloth extra, 3s. 6d. each; post 8vo, Illustrated boards, 2s. each.
The Lost Heiress : A Tale of Love, Battle, and Adventure. With Two Illustrations by H. NISBET.
The Fossicker : A Romance of Mashonaland. With Two Illustrations by HUME NISBET.
A Fair Colonist. With a Frontispiece by STANLEY WOOD.

The Golden Rock. With a Frontispiece by STANLEY WOOD. Crown 8vo, cloth extra, 3s. 6d.
Kloof Yarns. Crown 8vo, picture cover, 1s.; cloth, 1s. 6d.
Tales from the Veld. With Twelve Illustrations by M. NISBET. Crown 8vo, cloth, 3s. 6d.

Glenny (George).—A Year's Work in Garden and Greenhouse:
Practical Advice as to the Management of the Flower, Fruit, and Frame Garden. Post 8vo, 1s.; cloth, 1s. 6d.

Godwin (William).—Lives of the Necromancers. Post 8vo, cl., 2s.

Golden Treasury of Thought, The: An Encyclopædia of QUOTA-
TIONS. Edited by THEODORE TAYLOR. Crown 8vo, cloth gilt, 7s. 6d.

Gontaut, Memoirs of the Duchesse de (Gouvernante to the Chil-
dren of France), 1773-1836. With Two Photogravures. Two Vols., demy 8vo, cloth extra, 21s.

Goodman (E. J.).—The Fate of Herbert Wayne. Cr. 8vo, 3s. 6d.

Greeks and Romans, The Life of the, described from Antique
Monuments. By ERNST GUHL and W. KONER. Edited by Dr. F. HUEFFER. With 545 Illustrations. Large crown 8vo, cloth extra, 7s. 6d.

Greville (Henry), Novels by.
Post 8vo, illustrated boards, 2s. each.
Nikanor. Translated by ELIZA E. CHASE.
A Noble Woman. Translated by ALBERT D. VANDAM.

Griffith (Cecil).—Corinthia Marazion : A Novel. Crown 8vo, cloth
extra, 3s. 6d.; post 8vo, Illustrated boards, 2s.

Grundy (Sydney).—The Days of his Vanity: A Passage in the
Life of a Young Man. Crown 8vo, cloth extra, 3s. 6d.; post 8vo, Illustrated boards, 2s.

Habberton (John, Author of ' Helen's Babies '), **Novels by.**
Post 8vo, Illustrated boards, 2s. each : cloth limp, 2s. 6d. each.
Brueton's Bayou. | Country Luck.

Hair, The: Its Treatment in Health, Weakness, and Disease. Translated from the German of Dr. J. PINCUS. Crown 8vo, 1s.; cloth, 1s. 6d.

Hake (Dr. Thomas Gordon), Poems by.   Cr. 8vo, cl. ex., 6s. each.
New Symbols. | Legends of the Morrow. | The Serpent Play.
Maiden Ecstasy. Small 4to, cloth extra, 8s.

Halifax (C.).—Dr. Rumsey's Patient.   By Mrs. L. T. MEADE and
CLIFFORD HALIFAX, M.D. Crown 8vo, cloth, 3s. 6d.

Hall (Mrs. S. C.).—Sketches of Irish Character. With numerous
Illustrations on Steel and Wood by MACLISE, GILBERT, HARVEY, and GEORGE CRUIKSHANK.
Small demy 8vo, cloth extra, 7s. 6d.

Hall (Owen), Novels by.
The Track of a Storm. Cheaper Edition. Crown 8vo, cloth, 3s. 6d.
Jetsam. Crown 8vo, cloth, 3s. 6d.

Halliday (Andrew).—Every-day Papers. Post 8vo, boards, 2s.

Handwriting, The Philosophy of. With over 100 Facsimiles and
Explanatory Text. By DON FELIX DE SALAMANCA. Post 8vo, cloth limp, 2s. 6d.

Hanky-Panky: Easy and Difficult Tricks, White Magic, Sleight of
Hand, &c. Edited by W. H. CREMER. With 200 Illustrations. Crown 8vo, cloth extra, 4s. 6d.

Hardy (Thomas).—Under the Greenwood Tree. Crown 8vo, cloth
extra, with Portrait and 15 Illustrations, 3s. 6d.; post 8vo, illustrated boards, 2s.; cloth limp, 2s. 6d.

Harte's (Bret) Collected Works. Revised by the Author. LIBRARY
EDITION, in Nine Volumes, crown 8vo, cloth extra, 6s. each.
Vol.   I. COMPLETE POETICAL AND DRAMATIC WORKS. With Steel-plate Portrait.
  „   II. THE LUCK OF ROARING CAMP—BOHEMIAN PAPERS—AMERICAN LEGEND.
  „ III. TALES OF THE ARGONAUTS—EASTERN SKETCHES.
  „   IV. GABRIEL CONROY. | Vol. V. STORIES—CONDENSED NOVELS, &c.
  „   VI. TALES OF THE PACIFIC SLOPE.
  „ VII. TALES OF THE PACIFIC SLOPE—II. With Portrait by JOHN PETTIE, R.A.
  „ VIII. TALES OF THE PINE AND THE CYPRESS.
  „   IX. BUCKEYE AND CHAPPAREL.

Bret Harte's Choice Works, in Prose and Verse. With Portrait of the Author and 40 Illustrations. Crown 8vo, cloth, 3s. 6d.
Bret Harte's Poetical Works. Printed on hand-made paper. Crown 8vo, buckram, 4s. 6d.
A New Volume of Poems. Crown 8vo, buckram, 5s.   [Preparing.
The Queen of the Pirate Isle. With 28 Original Drawings by KATE GREENAWAY reproduced in Colours by EDMUND EVANS. Small 4to, cloth, 5s.
                    Crown 8vo, cloth extra, 3s. 6d. each ; post 8vo, picture boards, 2s. each.
A Waif of the Plains. With 60 Illustrations by STANLEY L. WOOD.
A Ward of the Golden Gate. With 59 Illustrations by STANLEY L. WOOD.
                    Crown 8vo, cloth extra, 3s. 6d. each.
A Sappho of Green Springs, &c. With Two Illustrations by HUME NISBET.
Colonel Starbottle's Client, and Some Other People. With a Frontispiece.
Susy : A Novel. With Frontispiece and Vignette by J. A. CHRISTIE.
Sally Dows, &c. With 47 Illustrations by W. D. ALMOND and others.
A Protegee of Jack Hamlin's, &c. With 26 Illustrations by W. SMALL and others.
The Bell-Ringer of Angel's, &c. With 39 Illustrations by DUDLEY HARDY and others.
Clarence : A Story of the American War. With Eight Illustrations by A. JULE GOODMAN.
Barker's Luck, &c. With 39 Illustrations by A. FORESTIER, PAUL HARDY, &c.
Devil's Ford, &c. With a Frontispiece by W. H. OVEREND.
The Crusade of the "Excelsior." With a Frontispiece by J. BERNARD PARTRIDGE.
Three Partners ; or, The Big Strike on Heavy Tree Hill. With 8 Illustrations by J. GULICH.
Tales of Trail and Town. With Frontispiece by G. P. JACOMB-HOOD.
                    Post 8vo, illustrated boards, 2s. each.
Gabriel Conroy. | **The Luck of Roaring Camp,** &c
An Heiress of Red Dog, &c. | **Californian Stories.**
                    Post 8vo, illustrated boards, 2s. each ; cloth, 2s. 6d. each.
Flip. | **Maruja.** | **A Phyllis of the Sierras.**

Haweis (Mrs. H. R.), Books by.
The Art of Beauty. With Coloured Frontispiece and 91 Illustrations. Square 8vo, cloth bds., 6s.
The Art of Decoration. With Coloured Frontispiece and 74 Illustrations. Sq. 8vo, cloth bds., 6s.
The Art of Dress. With 32 Illustrations. Post 8vo, 1s. ; cloth, 1s. 6d.
Chaucer for Schools. Demy 8vo, cloth limp, 2s. 6d.
Chaucer for Children. With 38 Illustrations (8 Coloured). Crown 4to, cloth extra, 3s. 6d.

Haweis (Rev. H. R., M.A.), Books by.
American Humorists : WASHINGTON IRVING, OLIVER WENDELL HOLMES, JAMES RUSSELL LOWELL, ARTEMUS WARD, MARK TWAIN, and BRET HARTE. Third Edition. Crown 8vo, cloth extra, 6s.
Travel and Talk, 1885-93-95 : My Hundred Thousand Miles of Travel through America—Canada—New Zealand—Tasmania—Australia—Ceylon—The Paradises of the Pacific. With Photogravure Frontispieces. A New Edition. Two Vols., crown 8vo, cloth, 12s.

Hawthorne (Julian), Novels by.
          Crown 8vo, cloth extra, 3s. 6d. each ; post 8vo, illustrated boards, 2s. each.
Garth. | **Ellice Quentin.** | **Beatrix Randolph.** With Four Illusts.
Sebastian Strome. | | **David Poindexter's Disappearance.**
Fortune's Fool. | **Dust.** Four Illusts. | **The Spectre of the Camera.**
                    Post 8vo, illustrated boards, 2s. each.
Miss Cadogna. | **Love—or a Name.**

Hawthorne (Nathaniel).—Our Old Home. Annotated with Passages from the Author's Note-books, and Illustrated with 31 Photogravures. Two Vols., cr. 8vo, 15s.

Helps (Sir Arthur), Works by. Post 8vo, cloth limp, 2s. 6d. each.
Animals and their Masters. | **Social Pressure.**
Ivan de Biron : A Novel. Crown 8vo, cloth extra, 3s. 6d. ; post 8vo, illustrated boards, 2s.

Henderson (Isaac). — Agatha Page : A Novel. Cr. 8vo. cl., 3s. 6d.

Henty (G. A.), Novels by.
Rujub the Juggler. With Eight Illustrations by STANLEY L. WOOD. Crown 8vo, cloth, 3s. 6d.; post 8vo, illustrated boards, 2s.
                    Crown 8vo, cloth, 3s. 6d. each.
Dorothy's Double. | **The Queen's Cup.**
Colonel Thorndyke's Secret. Crown 8vo, cloth, gilt top, 6s.

Herman (Henry).—A Leading Lady. Post 8vo, bds., 2s. ; cl., 2s. 6d.

Herrick's (Robert) Hesperides, Noble Numbers, and Complete
Collected Poems. With Memorial-Introduction and Notes by the Rev. A. B. GROSART, D.D., Steel Portrait, &c. Three Vols., crown 8vo, cloth boards, 3s. 6d. each.

Hertzka (Dr. Theodor).—Freeland: A Social Anticipation. Translated by ARTHUR RANSOM. Crown 8vo, cloth extra, 6s.

Hesse-Wartegg (Chevalier Ernst von).— Tunis: The Land and the People. With 22 Illustrations. Crown 8vo, cloth extra, 3s. 6d.

Hill (Headon).—Zambra the Detective. Crown 8vo, cloth, 3s. 6d. ; post 8vo, picture boards, 2s. : cloth, 2s. 6d.

Hill (John), Works by.

Treason-Felony. Post 8vo, boards, 2s. | The Common Ancestor. Cr. 8vo, cloth, 3s. 6d.

Hoey (Mrs. Cashel).—The Lover's Creed. Post 8vo, boards, 2s.

Holiday, Where to go for a. By E. P. SHOLL, Sir H. MAXWELL, Bart., M.P., JOHN WATSON, JANE BARLOW, MARY LOVETT CAMERON, JUSTIN H. MCCARTHY, PAUL LANGE, J. W. GRAHAM, J. H. SALTER, PHŒBE ALLEN, S. J. BECKETT, L. RIVERS VINE, and C. F. GORDON CUMMING. Crown 8vo, 1s. ; cloth, 1s. 6d.

Hollingshead (John).—Niagara Spray. Crown 8vo, 1s.

Holmes (Gordon, M.D.)—The Science of Voice Production and Voice Preservation. Crown 8vo, 2s. ; cloth, 1s. 6d.

Holmes (Oliver Wendell), Works by.

The Autocrat of the Breakfast-Table. Illustrated by J. GORDON THOMSON. Post 8vo, cloth limp, 2s. 6d.— Another Edition, post 8vo, cloth, 2s.

The Autocrat of the Breakfast-Table and The Professor at the Breakfast-Table In One Vol. Post 8vo, half-bound, 2s.

Hood's (Thomas) Choice Works in Prose and Verse. With Life of the Author, Portrait, and 200 Illustrations. Crown 8vo, cloth, 3s. 6d.

Hood's Whims and Oddities. With 85 Illustrations. Post 8vo, half-bound, 2s.

Hood (Tom).—From Nowhere to the North Pole: A Noah's Ark.ological Narrative. With 25 Illustrations by W. BRUNTON and E. C. BARNES. Cr. 8vo, cloth, 6s.

Hook's (Theodore) Choice Humorous Works; including his Ludi- crous Adventures, Bons Mots, Puns, and Hoaxes. With Life of the Author, Portraits, Facsimiles and Illustrations. Crown 8vo, cloth extra, 7s. 6d.

Hooper (Mrs. Geo.).—The House of Raby. Post 8vo, boards, 2s.

Hopkins (Tighe).—''Twixt Love and Duty.' With a Frontispiece. Crown 8vo, cloth, 3s. 6d.

Horne (R. Hengist). — Orion: An Epic Poem. With Photograph Portrait by SUMMERS. Tenth Edition. Crown 8vo, cloth extra, 7s.

Hungerford (Mrs., Author of ' Molly Bawn '), **Novels by.**

Post 8vo, Illustrated boards, 2s. each ; cloth limp, 2s. 6d. each.

A Maiden All Forlorn. | A Modern Circe. | An Unsatisfactory Lover.
Marvel. | A Mental Struggle. | Lady Patty.
In Durance Vile.

Crown 8vo, cloth extra, 3s. 6d. each; post 8vo, illustrated boards, 2s. each ; cloth limp, 2s. 6d. each.

Lady Verner's Flight.   The Professor's Experiment.
The Red-House Mystery.   Nora Creina.
The Three Graces.

Crown 8vo, cloth extra, 3s. 6d. each.

An Anxious Moment. | A Point of Conscience.
April's Lady. | Peter's Wife.

Lovice. Crown 8vo, cloth, 6s.

Hunt's (Leigh) Essays: A Tale for a Chimney Corner, &c. Edited by EDMUND OLLIER. Post 8vo, half-bound, 2s.

Hunt (Mrs. Alfred), Novels by.

Crown 8vo, cloth extra, 3s. 6d. each ; post 8vo, illustrated boards, 2s. each.

The Leaden Casket. | Self-Condemned. | That Other Person.

Thornicroft's Model. Post 8vo, boards, 2s. | Mrs. Juliet. Crown 8vo, cloth extra, 3s. 6d.

Hutchison (W. M.).—Hints on Colt-breaking. With 25 Illustra- tions. Crown 8vo, cloth extra, 3s. 6d.

Hydrophobia: An Account of M. PASTEUR's System ; The Technique of his Method, and Statistics. By RENAUD SUZOR, M.B. Crown 8vo, cloth extra, 6s.

Hyne (C. J. Cutcliffe).— Honour of Thieves. Cr. 8vo, cloth, 3s. 6d.

Impressions (The) of Aureole. Cheaper Edition, with a New Preface. Post 8vo, blush-rose paper and cloth, 2s. 6d.

Indoor Paupers. By ONE OF THEM. Crown 8vo, cloth, 1s. 6d.

Innkeeper's Handbook (The) and Licensed Victualler's Manual.
By J. TREVOR-DAVIES. Crown 8vo, 1s.; cloth, 1s. 6d.

Irish Wit and Humour, Songs of. Collected and Edited by A.
PERCEVAL GRAVES. Post 8vo, cloth limp, 2s. 6d.

Irving (Sir Henry): A Record of over Twenty Years at the Lyceum.
By PERCY FITZGERALD. With Portrait. Crown 8vo, 1s.; cloth, 1s. 6d.

James (C. T. C.):— A Romance of the Queen's Hounds. Post
8vo, cloth limp, 1s. 6d.

Jameson (William).—My Dead Self. Post 8vo, bds., 2s.; cl., 2s. 6d.

Japp (Alex. H., LL.D.).—Dramatic Pictures, &c. Cr. 8vo, cloth, 5s.

Jay (Harriett), Novels by. Post 8vo, illustrated boards, 2s. each.
The Dark Colleen. | The Queen of Connaught.

Jefferies (Richard), Works by. Post 8vo, cloth limp, 2s. 6d. each.
Nature near London. | The Life of the Fields. | The Open Air.
. Also the HAND-MADE PAPER EDITION, crown 8vo, buckram, gilt top, 6s. each.

The Eulogy of Richard Jefferies. By Sir WALTER BESANT. With a Photograph Portrait.
Crown 8vo, cloth extra, 6s.

Jennings (Henry J.), Works by.
Curiosities of Criticism. Post 8vo, cloth limp, 2s. 6d.
Lord Tennyson: A Biographical Sketch. With Portrait. Post 8vo, 1s.; cloth, 1s. 6d.

Jerome (Jerome K.), Books by.
Stageland. With 64 Illustrations by J. BERNARD PARTRIDGE. Fcap. 4to, picture cover, 1s.
John Ingerfield, &c. With 9 Illusts. by A. S. BOYD and JOHN GULICH. Fcap. 8vo; pic. cov: 1s. 6d.
The Prude's Progress: A Comedy by J. K. JEROME and EDEN PHILLPOTTS. Cr. 8vo, 1s. 6d.

**Jerrold (Douglas).—The Barber's Chair; and The Hedgehog
Letters.** Post 8vo, printed on laid paper and half-bound, 2s.

Jerrold (Tom), Works by. Post 8vo, 1s. ea.; cloth limp, 1s. 6d. each.
The Garden that Paid the Rent.
Household Horticulture: A Gossip about Flowers. Illustrated.

Jesse (Edward).—Scenes and Occupations of a Country·Life.
Post 8vo, cloth limp, 2s.

Jones (William, F.S.A.), Works by. Cr. 8vo, cl. extra, 7s. 6d. each.
Finger-Ring Lore: Historical, Legendary, and Anecdotal. With nearly 300 Illustrations. Second
Edition, Revised and Enlarged.
Credulities, Past and Present. Including the Sea and Seamen, Miners, Talismans, Word and
Letter Divination, Exorcising and Blessing of Animals, Birds, Eggs, Luck, &c. With Frontispiece.
Crowns and Coronations: A History of Regalia. With 100 Illustrations.

Jonson's (Ben) Works. With Notes Critical and Explanatory, and
a Biographical Memoir by WILLIAM GIFFORD. Edited by Colonel CUNNINGHAM. Three Vols,
crown 8vo, cloth extra, 3s. 6d. each.

Josephus, The Complete Works of. Translated by WHISTON. Con-
taining 'The Antiquities of the Jews' and 'The Wars of the Jews.' With 52 Illustrations and Maps.
Two Vols., demy 8vo, half-bound, 12s. 6d.

Kempt (Robert).—Pencil and Palette: Chapters on Art and Artists.
Post 8vo, cloth limp, 2s. 6d.

Kershaw (Mark). — Colonial Facts and Fictions: Humorous
Sketches. Post 8vo, illustrated boards, 2s.; cloth, 2s. 6d.

King (R. Ashe), Novels by.
Post 8vo, illustrated boards, 2s. each.
'The Wearing of the Green.' | Passion's Slave,
A Drawn Game. | Bell Barry,

Knight (William, M.R.C.S., and Edward, L.R.C.P.). — The
Patient's Vade Mecum: How to Get Most Benefit from Medical Advice. Cr. 8vo, 1s.; cl., 1s. 6d.

Knights (The) of the Lion: A Romance of the Thirteenth Century.
Edited, with an Introduction, by the MARQUESS OF LORNE, K.T. Crown 8vo, cloth extra, 6s.

Lamb's (Charles) Complete Works in Prose and Verse, including
'Poetry for Children' and 'Prince Dorus.' Edited, with Notes and Introduction, by R. H. SHEP-
HERD. With Two Portraits and Facsimile of the 'Essay on Roast Pig.' Crown 8vo, cloth, 3s. 6d.
The Essays of Elia. Post 8vo, printed on laid paper and half-bound, 2s.
Little Essays: Sketches and Characters by CHARLES LAMB, selected from his Letters by PERCY
FITZGERALD. Post 8vo, cloth limp, 2s. 6d.
The Dramatic Essays of Charles Lamb. With Introduction and Notes by BRANDER MAT-
THEWS, and Steel-plate Portrait. Fcap. 8vo, half-bound, 2s. 6d.

Landor (Walter Savage).—Citation and Examination of William
Shakspeare &c., before Sir Thomas Lucy, touching Deer-stealing, 19th September, 1582. To which
is added, A Conference of Master Edmund Spenser with the Earl of Essex, touching the
State of Ireland, 1595. Fcap. 8vo, half-Roxburghe, 2s. 6d.

Lane (Edward William).—The Thousand and One Nights, com-
monly called in England The Arabian Nights' Entertainments. Translated from the Arabic,
with Notes. Illustrated with many hundred Engravings from Designs by HARVEY. Edited by EDWARD
STANLEY POOLE. With Preface by STANLEY LANE-POOLE. Three Vols., demy 8vo, cloth, 7s. 6d. ea.

Larwood (Jacob), Works by.
Anecdotes of the Clergy. Post 8vo, laid paper, half-bound, 2s.

Post 8vo, cloth limp, 2s. 6d. each.
Forensic Anecdotes. | **Theatrical Anecdotes.**

Lehmann (R. C.), Works by. Post 8vo, 1s. each; cloth, 1s. 6d. each.
Harry Fludyer at Cambridge.
Conversational Hints for Young Shooters: A Guide to Polite Talk.

Leigh (Henry S.).—Carols of Cockayne. Printed on hand-made
paper, bound in buckram, 5s.

Leland (C. Godfrey). — A Manual of Mending and Repairing.
With Diagrams. Crown 8vo, cloth, 5s.

Lepelletier (Edmond). — Madame Sans-Gène. Translated from
the French by JOHN DE VILLIERS. Crown 8vo, cloth, 3s. 6d. ; post 8vo, picture boards, 2s.

Leys (John).—The Lindsays: A Romance. Post 8vo, illust. bds., 2s.

Lindsay (Harry).—Rhoda Roberts: A Welsh Mining Story. Crown
8vo, cloth, 3s. 6d.

Linton (E. Lynn), Works by.
Crown 8vo, cloth extra, 3s. 6d. each ; post 8vo, illustrated boards, 2s. each.
Patricia Kemball. | Ione.   **Under which Lord ?** With 12 Illustrations.
The Atonement of Leam Dundas.   **'My Love!' | Sowing the Wind.**
The World Well Lost. With 12 Illusts.   **Paston Carew,** Millionaire and Miser.
The One Too Many.   **Dulcie Everton.**

Post 8vo, illustrated boards, 2s. each.
The Rebel of the Family.   **With a Silken Thread.**

Post 8vo, cloth limp, 2s. 6d. each.
Witch Stories. | **Ourselves:** Essays on Women.
Freeshooting: Extracts from the Works of Mrs. LYNN LINTON.

Lucy (Henry W.).—Gideon Fleyce: A Novel. Crown 8vo, cloth
extra, 3s. 6d. ; post 8vo, illustrated boards, 2s.

Macalpine (Avery), Novels by.
Teresa Itasca. Crown 8vo, cloth extra, 1s
Broken Wings. With Six Illustrations by W. J. HENNESSY. Crown 8vo, cloth extra, 6s.

MacColl (Hugh), Novels by.
Mr. Stranger's Sealed Packet. Post 8vo, illustrated boards, 2s.
Ednor Whitlook. Crown 8vo, cloth extra, 6s.

Macdonell (Agnes).—Quaker Cousins. Post 8vo, boards, 2s.

MacGregor (Robert).—Pastimes and Players: Notes on Popular
Games. Post 8vo, cloth limp, 2s. 6d.

Mackay (Charles, LL.D.). — Interludes and Undertones; or,
Music at Twilight. Crown 8vo, cloth extra, 6s.

McCarthy (Justin, M.P.), Works by.

A History of Our Own Times, from the Accession of Queen Victoria to the General Election of 1880. LIBRARY EDITION. Four Vols., demy 8vo, cloth extra, 12s. each.—Also a POPULAR EDITION, in Four Vols., crown 8vo, cloth extra, 6s. each.—And the JUBILEE EDITION, with an Appendix of Events to the end of 1886, in Two Vols., large crown 8vo, cloth extra, 7s. 6d. each.
A History of Our Own Times, from 1880 to the Diamond Jubilee. Demy 8vo, cloth extra, 12s. Uniform with the LIBRARY EDITION of the first Four Volumes.
A Short History of Our Own Times. One Vol., crown 8vo, cloth extra, 6s.—Also a CHEAP POPULAR EDITION, post 8vo, cloth limp, 2s. 6d.
A History of the Four Georges. Four Vols., demy 8vo, cl. ex., 12s. each. [Vols. I. & II. ready.

Crown 8vo, cloth extra, 3s. 6d. each; post 8vo, illustrated boards, 2s. each; cloth limp, 2s. 6d. each.

The Waterdale Neighbours.	**Donna Quixote.** With 12 Illustrations.
My Enemy's Daughter.	**The Comet of a Season.**
A Fair Saxon.	**Maid of Athens.** With 12 Illustrations.
Linley Rochford.	**Camiola:** A Girl with a Fortune.
Dear Lady Disdain.	**The Dictator.**
Miss Misanthrope. With 12 Illustrations.	**Red Diamonds.**	**The Riddle Ring.**

The Three Disgraces, and other Stories. Crown 8vo, cloth, 3s. 6d.

'The Right Honourable.' By JUSTIN McCARTHY, M.P., and Mrs. CAMPBELL PRAED. Crown 8vo, cloth extra, 6s.

McCarthy (Justin Huntly), Works by.

The French Revolution. (Constituent Assembly, 1789-91). Four Vols., demy 8vo, cloth, 12s. each.
An Outline of the History of Ireland. Crown 8vo, 1s.; cloth, 1s. 6d.
Ireland Since the Union: Sketches of Irish History, 1798-1886. Crown 8vo, cloth, 6s.

Hafiz in London: Poems. Small 8vo, gold cloth, 3s. 6d.

Our Sensation Novel. Crown 8vo, picture cover, 1s.; cloth limp, 1s. 6d.
Doom! An Atlantic Episode. Crown 8vo, picture cover, 1s.
Dolly: A Sketch. Crown 8vo, picture cover, 1s.; cloth limp, 1s. 6d.
Lily Lass: A Romance. Crown 8vo, picture cover, 1s.; cloth limp, 1s. 6d.
The Thousand and One Days. With Two Photogravures. Two Vols., crown 8vo, half-bd., 12s.
A London Legend. Crown 8vo, cloth, 3s. 6d.
The Royal Christopher. Crown 8vo, cloth, 3s. 6d.

MacDonald (George, LL.D.), Books by.

Works of Fancy and Imagination. Ten Vols., 16mo, cloth, gilt edges, in cloth case, 21s.; or the Volumes may be had separately, in Grolier cloth, at 2s. 6d. each.
Vol. I. WITHIN AND WITHOUT.—THE HIDDEN LIFE.
  „ II. THE DISCIPLE.—THE GOSPEL WOMEN.—BOOK OF SONNETS.—ORGAN SONGS.
  „ III. VIOLIN SONGS.—SONGS OF THE DAYS AND NIGHTS.—A BOOK OF DREAMS.—ROADSIDE POEMS.—POEMS FOR CHILDREN.
  „ IV. PARABLES.—BALLADS.—SCOTCH SONGS.
  „ V. & VI. PHANTASTES: A Faerie Romance. | Vol. VII. THE PORTENT.
  „ VIII. THE LIGHT PRINCESS.—THE GIANT'S HEART.—SHADOWS.
  „ IX. CROSS PURPOSES.—THE GOLDEN KEY.—THE CARASOYN.—LITTLE DAYLIGHT.
  „ X. THE CRUEL PAINTER.—THE WOW O' RIVVEN.—THE CASTLE.—THE BROKEN SWORDS. —THE GRAY WOLF.—UNCLE CORNELIUS.

Poetical Works of George MacDonald. Collected and Arranged by the Author. Two Vols. crown 8vo, buckram, 12s.
A Threefold Cord. Edited by GEORGE MACDONALD. Post 8vo, cloth, 5s.

Phantastes: A Faerie Romance. With 25 Illustrations by J. BELL. Crown 8vo, cloth extra, 3s. 6d.
Heather and Snow: A Novel. Crown 8vo, cloth extra, 3s. 6d.; post 8vo, illustrated boards, 2s.
Lilith: A Romance. SECOND EDITION. Crown 8vo, cloth extra, 6s.

Maclise Portrait Gallery (The) of Illustrious Literary Charac-
ters: 85 Portraits by DANIEL MACLISE; with Memoirs—Biographical, Critical, Bibliographical, and Anecdotal—illustrative of the Literature of the former half of the Present Century, by WILLIAM BATES, B.A. Crown 8vo, cloth extra, 3s. 6d.

Macquoid (Mrs.), Works by. Square 8vo, cloth extra, 6s. each.
In the Ardennes. With 50 Illustrations by THOMAS R. MACQUOID.
Pictures and Legends from Normandy and Brittany. 34 Illusts. by T. R. MACQUOID.
Through Normandy. With 90 Illustrations by T. R. MACQUOID, and a Map.
Through Brittany. With 35 Illustrations by T. R. MACQUOID, and a Map.
About Yorkshire. With 67 Illustrations by T. R. MACQUOID.

Post 8vo, illustrated boards, 2s. each.

The Evil Eye, and other Stories.	**Lost Rose**, and other Stories.

Magician's Own Book, The: Performances with Eggs, Hats, &c.
Edited by W. H. CREMER. With 200 Illustrations. Crown 8vo, cloth extra, 4s. 6d.

Magic Lantern, The, and its Management : Including full Practical
Directions. By T. C. HEPWORTH. With 10 Illustrations. Crown 8vo, 1s.; cloth, 1s. 6d.

Magna Charta: An Exact Facsimile of the Original in the British
Museum, 3 feet by 2 feet, with Arms and Seals emblazoned in Gold and Colours, 5s.

Mallory (Sir Thomas). — Mort d'Arthur: The Stories of King
Arthur and of the Knights of the Round Table. (A Selection.) Edited by B. MONTGOMERIE RAN-KING. Post 8vo, cloth limp, 2s.

Mallock (W. H.), Works by.

The New Republic. Post 8vo, picture cover, 2s.; cloth limp, 2s. 6d.
The New Paul & Virginia: Positivism on an Island. Post 8vo, cloth, 2s. 6d.
A Romance of the Nineteenth Century. Crown 8vo, cloth 6s.; post 8vo, illust. boards, 2s.

Poems. Small 4to, parchment, 8s.
Is Life Worth Living? Crown 8vo, cloth extra, 6s.

Margueritte (Paul and Victor).—The Disaster. Translated by
FREDERIC LEES. Crown 8vo, cloth, 3s. 6d.

Marlowe's Works. Including his Translations. Edited, with Notes
and Introductions, by Colonel CUNNINGHAM. Crown 8vo, cloth extra, 3s. 6d.

Massinger's Plays. From the Text of WILLIAM GIFFORD. Edited
by Col. CUNNINGHAM. Crown 8vo, cloth extra, 3s. 6d.

Masterman (J.).—Half-a-Dozen Daughters. Post 8vo, boards, 2s.

Matthews (Brander).—A Secret of the Sea, &c. Post 8vo, illus-
trated boards, 2s.; cloth limp, 2s. 6d.

Meade (L. T.), Novels by.

A Soldier of Fortune. Crown 8vo, cloth, 3s. 6d.; post 8vo, illustrated boards, 2s.

Crown 8vo, cloth, 3s. 6d each.
In an Iron Grip. | **The Voice of the Charmer.** With 8 Illustrations.
Dr. Rumsey's Patient. By L. T. MEADE and CLIFFORD HALIFAX, M.D.

Merrick (Leonard), Novels by.

The Man who was Good. Post 8vo, picture boards, 2s.

Crown 8vo, cloth, 3s. 6d. each.
This Stage of Fools. | **Cynthia:** A Daughter of the Philistines.

Mexican Mustang (On a), through Texas to the Rio Grande. By
A. E. SWEET and J. ARMOY KNOX. With 265 Illustrations. Crown 8vo, cloth extra, 7s. 6d.

Middlemass (Jean), Novels by. Post 8vo, illust. boards, 2s. each.
Touch and Go. | **Mr. Dorillion.**

Miller (Mrs. F. Fenwick).—Physiology for the Young; or, The
House of Life. With numerous Illustrations. Post 8vo, cloth limp, 2s. 6d.

Milton (J. L.), Works by. Post 8vo, 1s. each; cloth, 1s. 6d. each.
The Hygiene of the Skin. With Directions for Diet, Soaps, Baths, Wines, &c.
The Bath in Diseases of the Skin.
The Laws of Life, and their Relation to Diseases of the Skin.

Minto (Wm.).—Was She Good or Bad? Cr. 8vo, 1s.; cloth, 1s. 6d.

Mitford (Bertram), Novels by. Crown 8vo, cloth extra, 3s. 6d. each.
The Gun-Runner: A Romance of Zululand. With a Frontispiece by STANLEY L. WOOD.
The Luck of Gerard Ridgeley. With a Frontispiece by STANLEY L. WOOD.
The King's Assegai. With Six full-page Illustrations by STANLEY L. WOOD.
Renshaw Fanning's Quest. With a Frontispiece by STANLEY L. WOOD.

Molesworth (Mrs.), Novels by.
Hathercourt Rectory. Post 8vo, illustrated boards, 2s.
That Girl in Black. Crown 8vo, cloth, 1s. 6d.

Moncrieff (W. D. Scott-).—The Abdication: An Historical Drama.
With Seven Etchings by JOHN PETTIE, W. Q. ORCHARDSON, J. MACWHIRTER, COLIN HUNTER,
R. MACBETH and TOM GRAHAM. Imperial 4to, buckram, 21s.

Moore (Thomas), Works by.
The Epicurean; and **Alciphron.** Post 8vo, half-bound, 2s.
Prose and Verse; including Suppressed Passages from the MEMOIRS OF LORD BYRON. Edited
by R. H. SHEPHERD. With Portrait. Crown 8vo, cloth extra, 7s. 6d.

Muddock (J. E.) Stories by.
Crown 8vo, cloth extra, 3s. 6d. each.
Maid Marian and Robin Hood. With 12 Illustrations by STANLEY WOOD.
Basile the Jester. With Frontispiece by STANLEY WOOD.
Young Lochinvar.

Post 8vo, illustrated boards, 2s. each.
The Dead Man's Secret. | **From the Bosom of the Deep.**
Stories Weird and Wonderful. Post 8vo, illustrated boards, 2s.; cloth, 2s. 6d.

Murray (D. Christie), Novels by.
Crown 8vo, cloth extra, 3s. 6d. each ; post 8vo, illustrated boards, 2s. each.

A Life's Atonement.	A Model Father.	Bob Martin's Little Girl.
Joseph's Coat. 12 Illusts.	Old Blazer's Hero.	Time's Revenges.
Coals of Fire. 3 Illusts.	Cynic Fortune. Frontisp.	A Wasted Crime.
Val Strange.	By the Gate of the Sea.	In Direst Peril.
Hearts.	A Bit of Human Nature.	Mount Despair.
The Way of the World.	First Person Singular.	A Capful o' Nails.

The Making of a Novelist : An Experiment in Autobiography, With a Collotype Portrait. Cr. 8vo, buckram, 3s. 6d.
My Contemporaries in Fiction. Crown 8vo, buckram, 3s. 6d.
This Little World. Crown 8vo, cloth, gilt top, 6s.
Tales in Prose and Verse. With Frontispiece by ARTHUR HOPKINS. Cr. 8vo, cloth, 3s. 6d.
A Race for Millions, Crown 8vo, cloth, 3s. 6d.

Murray (D. Christie) and Henry Herman, Novels by.
Crown 8vo, cloth extra, 3s. 6d. each ; post 8vo, illustrated boards, 2s. each.
One Traveller Returns. | The Bishops' Bible.
Paul Jones's Alias, &c. With Illustrations by A. FORESTIER and G. NICOLET.

Murray (Henry), Novels by.
Post 8vo, illustrated boards, 2s. each : cloth, 2s. 6d. each.
A Game of Bluff. | A Song of Sixpence.

Newbolt (Henry).—Taken from the Enemy. Fcp. 8vo, cloth, 1s. 6d.

Nisbet (Hume), Books by.
'Ball Up.' Crown 8vo, cloth extra, 3s. 6d. ; post 8vo, illustrated boards, 2s.
Dr. Bernard St. Vincent. Post 8vo, illustrated boards, 2s.
Lessons in Art. With 21 Illustrations. Crown 8vo, cloth extra, 2s. 6d.

Norris (W. E.), Novels by.
Saint Ann's. Crown 8vo, cloth, 3s. 6d. ; post 8vo, picture boards, 2s.
Billy Bellew. With a Frontispiece by F. H. TOWNSEND. Crown 8vo, cloth, 3s. 6d.

O'Hanlon (Alice), Novels by. Post 8vo, illustrated boards, 2s. each.
The Unforeseen. | Chance ? or Fate ?

Ohnet (Georges), Novels by. Post 8vo, illustrated boards, 2s. each.
Doctor Rameau. | A Last Love.
A Weird Gift. Crown 8vo, cloth, 3s. 6d. ; post 8vo, picture boards, 2s.

Oliphant (Mrs.), Novels by. Post 8vo, illustrated boards, 2s. each.
The Primrose Path. | Whiteladies.
The Greatest Heiress in England.
The Sorceress. Crown 8vo, cloth, 3s. 6d.

O'Reilly (Mrs.).—Phœbe's Fortunes. Post 8vo, illust. boards, 2s.

O'Shaughnessy (Arthur), Poems by :
Fcap. 8vo, cloth extra, 7s. 6d. each.
Music and Moonlight. | Songs of a Worker.
Lays of France. Crown 8vo, cloth extra, 10s. 6d.

Ouida, Novels by. Cr. 8vo, cl., 3s. 6d. ea.; post 8vo, illust. bds., 2s. ea.

Held in Bondage.	Folle-Farine.	Moths.	Pipistrello.
Tricotrin.	A Dog of Flanders.	In Maremma.	Wanda.
Strathmore.	Pascarel.	Signa.	Bimbi.	Syrlin.
Chandos.	Two Wooden Shoes.	Frescoes.	Othmar.
Cecil Castlemaine's Gage	In a Winter City.	Princess Napraxine.
Under Two Flags.	Ariadne.	Friendship.	Guilderoy.	Ruffino.
Puck.	Idalia.	A Village Commune.	Two Offenders.

Bimbi. With Nine Illustrations by EDMUND H. GARRETT. Square 8vo, cloth extra, 5s.
Santa Barbara, &c. Square 8vo, cloth, 6s. ; crown 8vo, cloth, 3s. 6d.; post 8vo, illustrated boards, 2s.
POPULAR EDITIONS. Medium 8vo, 6d. each; cloth, 1s. each.
Under Two Flags. | Moths.
Under Two Flags and Moths. POPULAR EDITION, in One Volume. Medium 8vo, cloth, 2s.
Wisdom, Wit, and Pathos, selected from the Works of OUIDA by F. SYDNEY MORRIS. Post 8vo, cloth extra, 5s.—CHEAP EDITION, illustrated boards, 2s.

Page (H. A.).—Thoreau: His Life and Aims. With Portrait. Post 8vo, cloth, 2s. 6d.

Pandurang Hari; or, Memoirs of a Hindoo. With Preface by Sir
BARTLE FRERE. Crown 8vo, cloth, 3s. 6d.; post 8vo, illustrated boards, 2s.

Parker (Rev. Joseph, D.D.).—Might Have Been: some Life
Notes. Crown 8vo, cloth, 6s.

Pascal's Provincial Letters. A New Translation, with Historical
Introduction and Notes by T. M'CRIE, D.D. Post 8vo, cloth limp, 2s.

Paul (Margaret A.).—Gentle and Simple. Crown 8vo, cloth, with
Frontispiece by HELEN PATERSON, 3s. 6d.; post 8vo, illustrated boards, 2s.

Payn (James), Novels by.
Crown 8vo, cloth extra, 3s. 6d. each; post 8vo, Illustrated boards, 2s. each.

Lost Sir Massingberd.
Walter's Word. | A County Family.
Less Black than We're Painted.
By Proxy. | For Cash Only.
High Spirits.
Under One Roof.
A Confidential Agent. With 12 Illusts.
A Grape from a Thorn. With 12 Illusts.

Holiday Tasks.
The Canon's Ward. With Portrait.
The Talk of the Town. With 12 Illusts.
Glow-Worm Tales.
The Mystery of Mirbridge.
The Word and the Will.
The Burnt Million.
Sunny Stories. | A Trying Patient.

Post 8vo illustrated boards, 2s. each.

Humorous Stories. | From Exile.
The Foster Brothers.
The Family Scapegrace.
Married Beneath Him.
Bentinck's Tutor.
A Perfect Treasure.
Like Father, Like Son.
A Woman's Vengeance.
Carlyon's Year. | Cecil's Tryst.
Murphy's Master. | At Her Mercy.

The Clyffards of Clyffe.
Found Dead. | Gwendoline's Harvest.
Mirk Abbey. | A Marine Residence.
Some Private Views.
Not Wooed, But Won.
Two Hundred Pounds Reward.
The Best of Husbands.
Halves. | What He Cost Her.
Fallen Fortunes. | Kit: A Memory.
A Prince of the Blood.

In Peril and Privation. With 17 Illustrations. Crown 8vo, cloth, 3s. 6d.
Notes from the 'News.' Crown 8vo, portrait cover, 1s.; cloth, 1s. 6d.

Payne (Will).—Jerry the Dreamer. Crown 8vo, cloth, 3s. 6d.

Pennell (H. Cholmondeley), Works by. Post 8vo, cloth, 2s. 6d. ea.
Puck on Pegasus. With Illustrations.
Pegasus Re-Saddled. With Ten full-page Illustrations by G. DU MAURIER.
The Muses of Mayfair: Vers de Société. Selected by H. C. PENNELL.

Phelps (E. Stuart), Works by. Post 8vo, 1s. ea.; cloth, 1s. 6d. ea.
Beyond the Gates. | An Old Maid's Paradise. | Burglars in Paradise.
Jack the Fisherman. Illustrated by C. W. REED. Crown 8vo, cloth, 1s. 6d.

Phil May's Sketch-Book. Containing 54 Humorous Cartoons. A
New Edition. Crown folio, cloth, 2s. 6d.

Phipson (Dr. T. L.).—Famous Violinists and Fine Violins:
Historical Notes, Anecdotes, and Reminiscences. Crown 8vo, cloth, 5s.

Planche (J. R.), Works by.
The Pursuivant of Arms. With Six Plates and 209 Illustrations. Crown 8vo, cloth, 7s. 6d.
Songs and Poems, 1819-1879. With Introduction by Mrs. MACKARNESS. Crown 8vo, cloth, 6s.

Plutarch's Lives of Illustrious Men. With Notes and a Life of
Plutarch by JOHN and WM. LANGHORNE, and Portraits. Two Vols., demy 8vo, half-bound 10s. 6d.

Poe's (Edgar Allan) Choice Works in Prose and Poetry. With Intro-
duction by CHARLES BAUDELAIRE. Portrait and Facsimiles. Crown 8vo, cloth, 7s. 6d.
The Mystery of Marie Roget, &c. Post 8vo, illustrated boards, 2s.

Pollock (W. H.).—The Charm, and other Drawing-room Plays. By
Sir WALTER BESANT and WALTER H. POLLOCK. With 50 Illustrations. Crown 8vo, cloth gilt, 6s.

Pollock (Wilfred).—War and a Wheel: The Græco-Turkish War as
Seen from a Bicycle. With a Map. Crown 8vo, picture cover, 1s.

Pope's Poetical Works. Post 8vo, cloth limp, 2s.

Porter (John).—Kingsclere. Edited by BYRON WEBBER. With 19
full-page and many smaller Illustrations. Second Edition. Demy 8vo, cloth decorated, 18s.

Praed (Mrs. Campbell), Novels by. Post 8vo, illust. bds., 2s. each.
The Romance of a Station. | The Soul of Countess Adrian.

Crown 8vo, cloth, 3s. 6d. each; post 8vo, boards, 2s. each.

Outlaw and Lawmaker. | Christina Chard. With Frontispiece by W. PAGET.
Mrs. Tregaskiss. With 8 Illustrations by ROBERT SAUBER.

Nulma: An Anglo-Australian Romance. Crown 8vo, cloth, 6s.

Price (E. C.), Novels by.
Crown 8vo, cloth extra, 3s. 6d. each; post 8vo, Illustrated boards, 2s. each.
Valentina. | The Foreigners. | Mrs. Lancaster's Rival.

Gerald. Post 8vo, Illustrated boards, 2s.

Princess Olga.—Radna: A Novel. Crown 8vo, cloth extra, 6s.

Proctor (Richard A.), Works by.

Flowers of the Sky. With 55 Illustrations. Small crown 8vo, cloth extra, 3*s.* 6*d.*
Easy Star Lessons. With Star Maps for every Night in the Year. Crown 8vo, cloth, 6*s.*
Familiar Science Studies. Crown 8vo, cloth extra, 6*s.*
Saturn and its System. With 13 Steel Plates. Demy 8vo, cloth extra, 10*s.* 6*d.*
Mysteries of Time and Space. With numerous Illustrations. Crown 8vo, cloth extra, 6*s.*
The Universe of Suns, &c. With numerous Illustrations. Crown 8vo, cloth extra, 6*s.*
Wages and Wants of Science Workers. Crown 8vo, 1*s.* 6*d.*

Pryce (Richard).—Miss Maxwell's Affections. Crown 8vo, cloth,
with Frontispiece by HAL LUDLOW, 3*s.* 6*d.*; post 8vo, illustrated boards, 2*s.*

Rambosson (J.).—Popular Astronomy. Translated by C. B. PIT-
MAN. With 10 Coloured Plates and 63 Woodcut Illustrations. Crown 8vo, cloth, 3*s.* 6*d.*

Randolph (Lieut.-Col. George, U.S.A.).—Aunt Abigail Dykes:
A Novel. Crown 8vo, cloth extra, 7*s.* 6*d.*

Read (General Meredith).—Historic Studies in Vaud, Berne,
and Savoy. With 31 full-page Illustrations. Two Vols., demy 8vo, cloth, 28*s.*

Reade's (Charles) Novels.

The New Collected LIBRARY EDITION, complete in Seventeen Volumes, set in new long primer type, printed on laid paper, and elegantly bound in cloth, price 3*s.* 6*d.* each.

1. **Peg Woffington; and Christie John-stone.**
2. **Hard Cash.**
3. **The Cloister and the Hearth.** With a Preface by Sir WALTER BESANT.
4. **'It is Never Too Late to Mend.'**
5. **The Course of True Love Never Did Run Smooth; and Singleheart and Doubleface.**
6. **The Autobiography of a Thief; Jack of all Trades; A Hero and a Martyr; and The Wandering Heir.**
7. **Love Me Little, Love me Long.**
8. **The Double Marriage.**
9. **Griffith Gaunt.**
10. **Foul Play.**
11. **Put Yourself in His Place.**
12. **A Terrible Temptation.**
13. **A Simpleton.**
14. **A Woman-Hater.**
15. **The Jilt, and other Stories; and Good Stories of Man and other Animals.**
16. **A Perilous Secret.**
17. **Readiana; and Bible Characters.**

In Twenty-one Volumes, post 8vo, illustrated boards, 2*s.* each.

Peg Woffington. | **Christie Johnstone.**
'It is Never Too Late to Mend.'
The Course of True Love Never Did Run Smooth.
The Autobiography of a Thief; Jack of all Trades; and James Lambert.
Love Me Little, Love Me Long.
The Double Marriage.
The Cloister and the Hearth.
Hard Cash. | **Griffith Gaunt.**
Foul Play. | **Put Yourself in His Place.**
A Terrible Temptation
A Simpleton. | **The Wandering Heir.**
A Woman-Hater.
Singleheart and Doubleface.
Good Stories of Man and other Animals.
The Jilt, and other Stories.
A Perilous Secret. | **Readiana.**

POPULAR EDITIONS, medium 8vo, 6*d.* each : cloth, 1*s.* each.
'It is Never Too Late to Mend.' | **The Cloister and the Hearth.**
Peg Woffington; and Christie Johnstone.

It is Never Too Late to Mend' and **The Cloister and the Hearth** in One Volume, medium 8vo, cloth, 1*s.*
Christie Johnstone. With Frontispiece. Choicely printed in Elzevir style. Fcap. 8vo, half-Roxb. 2*s.* 6*d.*
Peg Woffington. Choicely printed in Elzevir style. Fcap. 8vo, half-Roxburghe, 2*s.* 6*d.*
The Cloister and the Hearth. In Four Vols., post 8vo, with an Introduction by Sir WALTER BESANT, and a Frontispiece to each Vol., 14*s.* the set.
Bible Characters. Fcap. 8vo, leatherette, 1*s.*
Selections from the Works of Charles Reade. With an Introduction by Mrs. ALEX. IRBLAND. Crown 8vo, buckram, with Portrait, 6*s.*; CHEAP EDITION, post 8vo, cloth limp, 2*s.* 6*d.*

Riddell (Mrs. J. H.), Novels by.

Weird Stories. Crown 8vo, cloth extra, 3*s.* 6*d.*; post 8vo, illustrated boards, 2*s.*

Post 8vo, illustrated boards, 2*s.* each.
The Uninhabited House. | **Fairy Water.**
The Prince of Wales's Garden Party. | **Her Mother's Darling.**
The Mystery in Palace Gardens. | **The Nun's Curse.** | **Idle Tales.**

Rimmer (Alfred), Works by. Square 8vo, cloth gilt, 7*s.* 6*d.* each.
Our Old Country Towns. With 55 Illustrations by the Author.
Rambles Round Eton and Harrow. With 50 Illustrations by the Author.
About England with Dickens. With 58 Illustrations by C. A. VANDERHOOF and A. RIMMER.

Rives (Amelie).—Barbara Dering. Crown 8vo, cloth extra, 3*s.* 6*d.*
post 8vo, illustrated boards, 2*s.*

Robinson Crusoe. By DANIEL DEFOE. With 37 Illustrations by
GEORGE CRUIKSHANK. Post 8vo, half-cloth, 2*s.*; cloth extra, gilt edges, 2*s.* 6*d.*

Robinson (F. W.), Novels by.

Women are Strange. Post 8vo, illustrated boards, 2*s.*
The Hands of Justice. Crown 8vo, cloth extra, 3*s.* 6*d.*; post 8vo, illustrated boards, 2*s.*
The Woman in the Dark. Crown 8vo, cloth, 3*s.* 6*d.* ; post 8vo, illustrated boards, 2*s.*

Robinson (Phil), Works by. Crown 8vo, cloth extra, 6s. each.
The Poets' Birds. | The Poets' Beasts.
The Poets and Nature: Reptiles, Fishes, and Insects.

Rochefoucauld's Maxims and Moral Reflections. With Notes
and an Introductory Essay by SAINTE-BEUVE. Post 8vo, cloth limp, 2s

Roll of Battle Abbey, The: A List of the Principal Warriors who
came from Normandy with William the Conqueror, 1066. Printed in Gold and Colours, 5s.

Rosengarten (A.).—A Handbook of Architectural Styles. Translated by W. COLLETT-SANDARS. With 630 Illustrations. Crown 8vo, cloth extra, 7s. 6d.

Rowley (Hon. Hugh), Works by. Post 8vo, cloth, 2s. 6d. each.
Puniana: Riddles and Jokes. With numerous Illustrations.
More Puniana. Profusely Illustrated.

Runciman (James), Stories by. Post 8vo, bds., 2s. ea.; cl., 2s. 6d. ea,
Skippers & Shellbacks. | Grace Balmaign's Sweetheart. | Schools & Scholars.

Russell (Dora), Novels by.
A Country Sweetheart. Crown 8vo, cloth, 3s. 6d.; post 8vo, picture boards, 2s.
The Drift of Fate. Crown 8vo, cloth, 3s. 6d.

Russell (Herbert).—True Blue; or, The Lass that Loved a Sailor.
Crown 8vo, cloth, 3s. 6d.

Russell (W. Clark), Novels, &c., by.
Crown 8vo, cloth extra, 3s. 6d. each; post 8vo, illustrated boards, 2s. each; cloth limp, 2s. 6d. each.
Round the Galley-Fire. | An Ocean Tragedy.
In the Middle Watch. | My Shipmate Louise.
On the Fo'k'sle Head. | Alone on a Wide Wide Sea.
A Voyage to the Cape. | The Good Ship 'Mohock.'
A Book for the Hammock. | The Phantom Death.
The Mystery of the 'Ocean Star.' | Is He the Man? | The Convict Ship.
The Romance of Jenny Harlowe. | Heart of Oak. |

Crown 8vo, cloth, 3s. 6d. each.
The Tale of the Ten. With 12 Illusts. by G. MONTBARD. | The Last Entry. Frontispiece.

Saint Aubyn (Alan), Novels by.
Crown 8vo, cloth extra, 3s. 6d. each; post 8vo, illustrated boards, 2s. each.
A Fellow of Trinity. With a Note by OLIVER WENDELL HOLMES and a Frontispiece.
The Junior Dean. | The Master of St. Benedict's. | To His Own Master.,
Orchard Damerel. | In the Face of the World. | The Tremlett Diamonds.

Fcap. 8vo, cloth boards, 1s. 6d. each.
The Old Maid's Sweetheart. | Modest Little Sara. |

Fortune's Gate. Crown 8vo, cloth, 6s.

Saint John (Bayle).—A Levantine Family. A New Edition.
Crown 8vo, cloth, 3s. 6d.

Sala (George A.).—Gaslight and Daylight. Post 8vo, boards, 2s.

Scotland Yard, Past and Present: Experiences of Thirty-seven Years.
By Ex-Chief-Inspector CAVANAGH. Post 8vo, illustrated boards, 2s.; cloth, 2s. 6d.

Secret Out, The: One Thousand Tricks with Cards; with Entertain-
ing Experiments in Drawing-room or 'White' Magic. By W. H. CREMER. With 300 Illustrations. Crown
8vo, cloth extra, 4s. 6d.

Seguin (L. G.), Works by.
The Country of the Passion Play (Oberammergau) and the Highlands of Bavaria. With
Map and 37 Illustrations. Crown 8vo, cloth extra, 3s. 6d.
Walks In Algiers. With Two Maps and 16 Illustrations. Crown 8vo, cloth extra, 6s.

Senior (Wm.).—By Stream and Sea. Post 8vo, cloth, 2s. 6d.

Sergeant (Adeline).—Dr. Endicott's Experiment. Cr. 8vo, 3s. 6d.

Shakespeare for Children: Lamb's Tales from Shakespeare.
With Illustrations, coloured and plain, by J. MOYR SMITH. Crown 4to, cloth gilt, 3s. 6d.

Shakespeare the Boy. With Sketches of the Home and School Life,
the Games and Sports, the Manners, Customs, and Folk-lore of the Time. By WILLIAM J. ROLFE,
Litt.D. With 42 Illustrations. Crown 8vo, cloth gilt, 3s. 6d.

Prose Works, in Two Vols.:
Vol. I. The Two Romances of Zastrozzi and St. Irvyne; the Dublin and Marlow Pamphlets; A Refutation of Deism; Letters to Leigh Hunt, and some Minor Writings and Fragments.
" II. The Essays; Letters from Abroad; Translations and Fragments, edited by Mrs. SHELLEY. With a Biography of Shelley, and an Index of the Prose Works.
. Also a few copies of a LARGE-PAPER EDITION, 5 vols., cloth, £2 12s. 6d.

Sherard (R. H.).—Rogues: A Novel. Crown 8vo, cloth, 1s. 6d.

Sheridan (General P. H.), Personal Memoirs of. With Portraits,
Maps, and Facsimiles. Two Vols., demy 8vo, cloth, 24s.

Sheridan's (Richard Brinsley) Complete Works, with Life and
Anecdotes. Including his Dramatic Writings, his Works in Prose and Poetry, Translations, Speeches, and Jokes. With 10 Illustrations. Crown 8vo, cloth, 3s. 6d.
The Rivals, The School for Scandal, and other Plays. Post 8vo, half-bound, 2s.
Sheridan's Comedies: The Rivals and **The School for Scandal.** Edited, with an Introduction and Notes to each Play, and a Biographical Sketch, by BRANDER MATTHEWS. With Illustrations. Demy 8vo, half-parchment, 12s. 6d.

Sidney's (Sir Philip) Complete Poetical Works, including all
those in 'Arcadia.' With Portrait, Memorial-Introduction, Notes, &c., by the Rev. A. B. GROSART, D.D. Three Vols., crown 8vo, cloth boards, 3s. 6d. each.

Signboards: Their History, including Anecdotes of Famous Taverns and
Remarkable Characters. By JACOB LARWOOD and JOHN CAMDEN HOTTEN. With Coloured Frontispiece and 94 Illustrations. Crown 8vo, cloth extra, 7s. 6d.

Sims (George R.), Works by.
Post 8vo, illustrated boards, 2s. each; cloth limp, 2s. 6d. each.

The Ring o' Bells.	**Dramas of Life.** With 60 Illustrations.
Mary Jane's Memoirs.	**Memoirs of a Landlady.**
Mary Jane Married.	**My Two Wives.**
Tinkletop's Crime.	**Scenes from the Show.**
Zeph: A Circus Story, &c.	**The Ten Commandments:** Stories.
Tales of To-day.	

Crown 8vo, picture cover, 1s. each; cloth, 1s. 6d. each.
The Dagonet Reciter and Reader: Being Readings and Recitations in Prose and Verse selected from his own Works by GEORGE R. SIMS.
The Case of George Candlemas. | **Dagonet Ditties.** (From *The Referee*.)

Rogues and Vagabonds. Crown 8vo, cloth, 3s. 6d.; post 8vo, picture boards, 2s.; cloth limp, 2s. 6d.
How the Poor Live; and Horrible London. Crown 8vo, picture cover, 1s
Dagonet Abroad. Crown 8vo, cloth, 3s. 6d.; post 8vo, picture boards, 2s.

Sister Dora: A Biography. By MARGARET LONSDALE. With Four
Illustrations. Demy 8vo, picture cover, 4d.; cloth, 6d.

Sketchley (Arthur).—A Match in the Dark. Post 8vo, boards, 2s.

Slang Dictionary (The): Etymological, Historical, and Anecdotal.
Crown 8vo, cloth extra, 6s. 6d.

Smart (Hawley), Novels by.
Crown 8vo, cloth 3s. 6d. each; post 8vo, picture boards, 2s. each.

Beatrice and Benedick.	**Long Odds.**
Without Love or Licence.	**The Master of Rathkelly.**

Crown 8vo, cloth, 3s. 6d. each.
The Outsider. | **A Racing Rubber.**
The Plunger. Post 8vo, picture boards, 2s.

Smith (J. Moyr), Works by.
The Prince of Argolis. With 130 Illustrations. Post 8vo, cloth extra, 3s. 6d.
The Wooing of the Water Witch. With numerous Illustrations. Post 8vo, cloth, 6s.

Society in London. Crown 8vo, 1s.; cloth, 1s. 6d.

Society in Paris: The Upper Ten Thousand. A Series of Letters
from Count PAUL VASILI to a Young French Diplomat. Crown 8vo, cloth, 6s.

Somerset (Lord Henry).—Songs of Adieu. Small 4to, Jap. vel., 6s.

Spalding (T. A., LL.B.).—Elizabethan Demonology: An Essay
on the Belief in the Existence of Devils. Crown 8vo, cloth extra, 5s.

Speight (T. W.), Novels by.

Post 8vo, illustrated boards, 2s. each.

The Mysteries of Heron Dyke. | The Loudwater Tragedy.
By Devious Ways, &c. | Burgo's Romance.
Hoodwinked; & Sandycroft Mystery. | Quittance in Full.
The Golden Hoop. | A Husband from the Sea.
Back to Life.

Post 8vo, cloth limp, 1s. 6d. each.

A Barren Title. | Wife or No Wife?

Crown 8vo, cloth extra, 3s. 6d. each.

A Secret of the Sea. | The Grey Monk. | The Master of Trenance.
A Minion of the Moon: A Romance of the King's Highway.
The Secret of Wyvern Towers.

Spenser for Children. By M. H. TOWRY. With Coloured Illustrations
by WALTER J. MORGAN. Crown 4to, cloth extra, 3s. 6d.

Spettigue (H. H.).—The Heritage of Eve. Crown 8vo, cloth, 6s.

Stafford (John), Novels by.
Doris and I. Crown 8vo, cloth, 3s. 6d.
Carlton Priors. Crown 8vo, cloth, gilt top,

Starry Heavens (The): A POETICAL BIRTHDAY BOOK. Royal 16mo,
cloth extra, 2s. 6d.

Stedman (E. C.), Works by. Crown 8vo, cloth extra, 9s. each.
Victorian Poets. | The Poets of America.

Stephens (Riccardo, M.B.).—The Cruciform Mark: The Strange
Story of RICHARD TREGENNA, Bachelor of Medicine (Univ. Edinb.) Crown 8vo, cloth, 3s. 6d.

Sterndale (R. Armitage).—The Afghan Knife: A Novel. Crown
8vo, cloth extra, 3s. 6d.; post 8vo, illustrated boards, 2s.

Stevenson (R. Louis), Works by. Post 8vo, cloth limp, 2s. 6d. ea.
Travels with a Donkey. With a Frontispiece by WALTER CRANE.
An Inland Voyage. With a Frontispiece by WALTER CRANE.

Crown 8vo, buckram, gilt top, 6s. each.

Familiar Studies of Men and Books.
The Silverado Squatters. With Frontispiece by J. D. STRONG.
The Merry Men. | Underwoods: Poems.
Memories and Portraits.
Virginibus Puerisque, and other Papers. | Ballads. | Prince Otto.
Across the Plains, with other Memories and Essays.
Weir of Hermiston.

A Lowden Sabbath Morn. With 27 full-page Illustrations by A. S. BOYD. Fcap. 4to,
cloth, 6s.
Songs of Travel. Crown 8vo, buckram, 5s.
New Arabian Nights. Crown 8vo, buckram, gilt top, 6s.; post 8vo, illustrated boards, 2s.
The Suicide Club; and The Rajah's Diamond. (From NEW ARABIAN NIGHTS.) With
Eight Illustrations by W. J. HENNESSY. Crown 8vo, cloth, 3s. 6d.
The Edinburgh Edition of the Works of Robert Louis Stevenson. Twenty-seven
Vols., demy 8vo. This Edition (which is limited to 1,000 copies) is sold in Sets only, the price of
which may be learned from the Booksellers. The First Volume was published Nov., 1894.

Stories from Foreign Novelists. With Notices by HELEN and
ALICE ZIMMERN. Crown 8vo, cloth extra, 3s. 6d.; post 8vo, illustrated boards, 2s.

Strange Manuscript (A) Found in a Copper Cylinder. Crown
8vo, cloth extra, with 19 Illustrations by GILBERT GAUL, 5s.; post 8vo, illustrated boards, 2s.

Strange Secrets. Told by PERCY FITZGERALD, CONAN DOYLE, FLOR-
ENCE MARRYAT, &c. Post 8vo, illustrated boards, 2s.

Strutt (Joseph). — The Sports and Pastimes of the People of
England; including the Rural and Domestic Recreations, May Games, Mummeries, Shows, &c., from
the Earliest Period to the Present Time. Edited by WILLIAM HONE. With 140 Illustrations. Crown
8vo, cloth extra, 3s. 6d.

Swift's (Dean) Choice Works, in Prose and Verse. With Memoir,
Portrait, and Facsimiles of the Maps in 'Gulliver's Travels.' Crown 8vo, cloth, 3s. 6d.
Gulliver's Travels, and A Tale of a Tub. Post 8vo, half-bound, 2s.
Jonathan Swift: A Study. By J. CHURTON COLLINS. Crown 8vo, cloth extra, 8s.

Swinburne (Algernon C.), Works by.

Selections from the Poetical Works of A. C. Swinburne. Fcap. 8vo 6s.
Atalanta in Calydon. Crown 8vo, 6s.
Chastelard: A Tragedy. Crown 8vo, 7s.
Poems and Ballads. FIRST SERIES. Crown 8vo, or fcap. 8vo, 9s.
Poems and Ballads. SECOND SERIES. Crown 8vo, 9s.
Poems & Ballads. THIRD SERIES. Cr. 8vo, 7s.
Songs before Sunrise. Crown 8vo, 10s. 6d.
Bothwell: A Tragedy. Crown 8vo, 12s. 6d.
Songs of Two Nations. Crown 8vo, 6s.
George Chapman. (See Vol. II. of G. CHAPMAN'S Works.) Crown 8vo, 3s. 6d.
Essays and Studies. Crown 8vo, 12s.
Erechtheus: A Tragedy. Crown 8vo, 6s.
A Note on Charlotte Bronte. Cr. 8vo, 6s.

A Study of Shakespeare. Crown 8vo, 8s.
Songs of the Springtides. Crown 8vo, 6s.
Studies in Song. Crown 8vo, 7s.
Mary Stuart: A Tragedy. Crown 8vo, 8s.
Tristram of Lyonesse. Crown 8vo, 9s.
A Century of Roundels. Small 4to, 8s.
A Midsummer Holiday. Crown 8vo, 7s.
Marino Faliero: A Tragedy. Crown 8vo, 6s.
A Study of Victor Hugo. Crown 8vo, 6s.
Miscellanies. Crown 8vo, 12s.
Locrine: A Tragedy. Crown 8vo, 6s.
A Study of Ben Jonson. Crown 8vo, 7s.
The Sisters: A Tragedy. Crown 8vo, 6s.
Astrophel, &c. Crown 8vo, 7s.
Studies in Prose and Poetry. Cr. 8vo, 9s.
The Tale of Balen. Crown 8vo, 7s.

Syntax's (Dr.) Three Tours: In Search of the Picturesque, in Search of Consolation, and in Search of a Wife. With ROWLANDSON'S Coloured Illustrations, and Life of the Author by J. C. HOTTEN. Crown 8vo, cloth extra, 7s. 6d.

Taine's History of English Literature. Translated by HENRY VAN LAUN. Four Vols., small demy 8vo, cloth boards, 30s.—POPULAR EDITION, Two Vols., large crown 8vo, cloth extra, 15s.

Taylor (Bayard). — Diversions of the Echo Club: Burlesques of Modern Writers. Post 8vo, cloth limp, 2s.

Taylor (Tom). — Historical Dramas. Containing 'Clancarty,' 'Jeanne Darc,' 'Twixt Axe and Crown,' 'The Fool's Revenge,' 'Arkwright's Wife,' 'Anne Boleyn,' 'Plot and Passion.' Crown 8vo, cloth extra, 7s. 6d.
*** The Plays may also be had separately, at 1s. each.

Tennyson (Lord): A Biographical Sketch. By H. J. JENNINGS. Post 8vo, portrait cover, 1s.; cloth, 1s. 6d.

Thackerayana: Notes and Anecdotes. With Coloured Frontispiece and Hundreds of Sketches by WILLIAM MAKEPEACE THACKERAY. Crown 8vo, cloth extra, 3s. 6d.

Thames, A New Pictorial History of the. By A. S. KRAUSSE. With 340 Illustrations. Post 8vo, cloth, 1s. 6d.

Thiers (Adolphe). — History of the Consulate and Empire of France under Napoleon. Translated by D. FORBES CAMPBELL and JOHN STEBBING. With 36 Steel Plates. 12 Vols., demy 8vo, cloth extra, 12s. each.

Thomas (Bertha), Novels by. Cr. 8vo, cl., 3s. 6d. ea.; post 8vo, 2s. ea.
The Violin-Player. | **Proud Maisie.**
Cressida. Post 8vo, illustrated boards, 2s.

Thomson's Seasons, and The Castle of Indolence. With Introduction by ALLAN CUNNINGHAM, and 48 Illustrations. Post 8vo, half-bound, 2s.

Thornbury (Walter), Books by.
The Life and Correspondence of J. M. W. Turner. With Eight Illustrations in Colours and Two Woodcuts. New and Revised Edition. Crown 8vo, cloth, 3s. 6d.
Post 8vo, illustrated boards, 2s. each.
Old Stories Re-told. | **Tales for the Marines.**

Timbs (John), Works by. Crown 8vo, cloth extra, 7s. 6d. each.
The History of Clubs and Club Life in London: Anecdotes of its Famous Coffee-houses, Hostelries, and Taverns. With 42 Illustrations.
English Eccentrics and Eccentricities: Stories of Delusions, Impostures, Sporting Scenes, Eccentric Artists, Theatrical Folk, &c. With 48 Illustrations.

Transvaal (The). By JOHN DE VILLIERS. With Map. Crown 8vo, 1s.

Trollope (Anthony), Novels by.
Crown 8vo, cloth extra, 3s. 6d. each; post 8vo, illustrated boards, 2s. each.
The Way We Live Now. | **Mr. Scarborough's Family.**
Frau Frohmann. | **The Land-Leaguers.**
Post 8vo, illustrated boards, 2s. each.
Kept in the Dark. | **The American Senator.**
The Golden Lion of Granpere. | **John Caldigate.** | **Marion Fay.**

Trollope (Frances E.), Novels by.
Crown 8vo, cloth extra, 3s. 6d. each; post 8vo, illustrated boards, 2s. each.
Like Ships Upon the Sea. | **Mabel's Progress.** | **Anne Furness.**

Trollope (T. A.).—Diamond Cut Diamond. Post 8vo, illust. bds., 2s.

Trowbridge (J. T.).—Farnell's Folly. Post 8vo, illust. boards, 2s.

Twain's (Mark) Books.

Crown 8vo, cloth extra, 3s. 6d. each.

The Choice Works of Mark Twain. Revised and Corrected throughout by the Author. With Life, Portrait, and numerous Illustrations.
Roughing It; and **The Innocents at Home.** With 200 Illustrations by F. A. FRASER.
The American Claimant. With 81 Illustrations by HAL HURST and others.
Tom Sawyer Abroad. With 26 Illustrations by DAN BEARD.
Tom Sawyer, Detective, &c. With Photogravure Portrait.
Pudd'nhead Wilson. With Portrait and Six Illllustrations by LOUIS LOEB.
Mark Twain's Library of Humour. With 197 Illustrations by E. W. KEMBLE.

Crown 8vo, cloth extra, 3s. 6d. each; post 8vo, picture boards, 2s. each,

A Tramp Abroad. With 314 Illustrations.
The Innocents Abroad; or, The New Pilgrim's Progress. With 234 Illustrations. (The Two Shilling Edition is entitled **Mark Twain's Pleasure Trip.)**
The Gilded Age. By MARK TWAIN and C. D. WARNER. With 212 Illustrations.
The Adventures of Tom Sawyer. With 111 Illustrations.
The Prince and the Pauper. With 190 Illustrations.
Life on the Mississippi. With 300 Illustrations.
The Adventures of Huckleberry Finn. With 174 Illustrations by E. W. KEMBLE.
A Yankee at the Court of King Arthur. With 220 Illustrations by DAN BEARD.
The Stolen White Elephant.
The £1,000,000 Bank-Note.

Mark Twain's Sketches. Post 8vo, illustrated boards, 2s.
Personal Recollections of Joan of Arc. With Twelve Illustrations by F. V. DU MOND. Crown 8vo, cloth, 6s.
More Tramps Abroad. Crown 8vo, cloth, gilt top, 6s.

Tytler (C. C. Fraser-).—Mistress Judith : A Novel. Crown 8vo, cloth extra, 3s. 6d. ; post 8vo, illustrated boards, 2s.

Tytler (Sarah), Novels by.

Crown 8vo, cloth extra, 3s. 6d. each ; post 8vo, illustrated boards, 2s. each

Lady Bell.	**Buried Diamonds.** | **The Blackhall Ghosts.**

Post 8vo, illustrated boards, 2s. each.

What She Came Through.	**The Huguenot Family.**
Citoyenne Jacqueline.	**Noblesse Oblige.**
The Bride's Pass.	**Beauty and the Beast.**
Saint Mungo's City.	**Disappeared.**

The Macdonald Lass. With Frontispiece. Crown 8vo, cloth, 3s. 6d.
The Witch-Wife. Crown 8vo, cloth, 3s. 6d.

Upward (Allen), Novels by.

A Crown of Straw. Crown 8vo, cloth, 6s.

Crown 8vo, cloth, 3s. 6d. each ; post 8vo, picture boards, 2s. each.

The Queen Against Owen.	**The Prince of Balkistan.**

'God Save the Queen!' a Tale of '37. Crown 8vo, decorated cover, 1s ; cloth, 2s.

Vashti and Esther. By 'Belle' of The World. Cr. 8vo, cloth, 3s. 6d.

Vizetelly (Ernest A.).—The Scorpion : A Romance of Spain. With a Frontispiece. Crown 8vo, cloth extra, 3s. 6d.

Walford (Edward, M.A.), Works by.

Walford's County Families of the United Kingdom (1898). Containing the Descent, Birth, Marriage, Education, &c., of 12,000 Heads of Families, their Heirs, Offices, Addresses, Clubs, &c. Royal 8vo, cloth gilt, 50s.
Walford's Shilling Peerage (1898). Containing a List of the House of Lords, Scotch and Irish Peers, &c. 32mo, cloth, 1s.
Walford's Shilling Baronetage (1898). Containing a List of the Baronets of the United Kingdom, Biographical Notices, Addresses, &c. 32mo, cloth, 1s.
Walford's Shilling Knightage (1898). Containing a List of the Knights of the United Kingdom, Biographical Notices, Addresses, &c. 32mo, cloth, 1s.
Walford's Shilling House of Commons (1898). Containing a List of all the Members of the New Parliament, their Addresses, Clubs, &c. 32mo, cloth, 1s.
Walford's Complete Peerage, Baronetage, Knightage, and House of Commons (1898). Royal 32mo, cloth, gilt edges, 5s.

Waller (S. E.).—Sebastiani's Secret. With Nine full-page Illustrations by the Author. Crown 8vo, cloth, 6s.

Walton and Cotton's Complete Angler; or, The Contemplative Man's Recreation, by IZAAK WALTON; and Instructions How to Angle, for a Trout or Grayling in a clear Stream, by CHARLES COTTON. With Memoirs and Notes by Sir HARRIS NICOLAS, and 61 Illustrations. Crown 8vo, cloth antique, 7s. 6d.

Walt Whitman, Poems by. Edited, with Introduction, by WILLIAM M. ROSSETTI. With Portrait. Crown 8vo, hand-made paper and buckram, 6s.

Ward (Herbert), Books by.
Five Years with the Congo Cannibals. With 92 Illustrations. Royal 8vo, cloth, 14s.
My Life with Stanley's Rear Guard. With Map. Post 8vo, 1s.; cloth, 1s. 6d.

Warman (Cy).—The Express Messenger, and other Tales of the Rail. Crown 8vo, cloth, 3s. 6d.

Warner (Charles Dudley).—A Roundabout Journey. Crown 8vo, cloth extra, 6s.

Warrant to Execute Charles I. A Facsimile, with the 59 Signatures and Seals. Printed on paper 22 in. by 14 in. 2s.
Warrant to Execute Mary Queen of Scots. A Facsimile, including Queen Elizabeth's Signature and the Great Seal. 2s.

Washington's (George) Rules of Civility Traced to their Sources and Restored by MONCURE D. CONWAY. Fcap. 8vo, Japanese vellum, 2s. 6d.

Wassermann (Lillias) and Aaron Watson.—The Marquis of Carabas. Post 8vo, illustrated boards, 2s.

Weather, How to Foretell the, with the Pocket Spectroscope. By F. W. CORY. With Ten Illustrations. Crown 8vo, 1s.; cloth, 1s. 6d.

Westall (William), Novels by.
Trust-Money. Post 8vo, illustrated boards, 2s.; cloth, 2s. 6d.
Sons of Belial. Crown 8vo, cloth extra, 3s. 6d.
With the Red Eagle: A Romance of the Tyrol. Crown 8vo, cloth, 6s.
A Woman Tempted Him. Crown 8vo, cloth, gilt top, 6s.

Westbury (Atha).—The Shadow of Hilton Fernbrook: A Ro- mance of Maoriland. Crown 8vo, cloth, 3s. 6d.

White (Gilbert).—The Natural History of Selborne. Post 8vo, printed on laid paper and half-bound, 2s.

Williams (W. Mattieu, F.R.A.S.), Works by.
Science in Short Chapters. Crown 8vo, cloth extra, 7s. 6d.
A Simple Treatise on Heat. With Illustrations. Crown 8vo, cloth, 2s. 6d.
The Chemistry of Cookery. Crown 8vo, cloth extra, 6s.
The Chemistry of Iron and Steel Making. Crown 8vo, cloth extra, 9s.
A Vindication of Phrenology. With Portrait and 43 Illusts. Demy 8vo, cloth extra, 12s. 6d.

Williamson (Mrs. F. H.).—A Child Widow. Post 8vo. bds., 2s.

Wills (C. J.), Novels by.
An Easy-going Fellow. Crown 8vo, cloth, 3s. 6d.
His Dead Past. Crown 8vo, cloth, 6s.

Wilson (Dr. Andrew, F.R.S.E.), Works by.
Chapters on Evolution. With 259 Illustrations. Crown 8vo, cloth extra, 7s. 6d.
Leaves from a Naturalist's Note-Book. Post 8vo, cloth limp, 2s. 6d.
Leisure-Time Studies. With Illustrations. Crown 8vo, cloth extra, 6s.
Studies in Life and Sense. With numerous Illustrations. Crown 8vo, cloth extra, 6s.
Common Accidents: How to Treat Them. With Illustrations. Crown 8vo, 1s.; cloth, 1s. 6d.
Glimpses of Nature. With 35 Illustrations. Crown 8vo, cloth extra, 3s. 6d.

Winter (John Strange), Stories by. Post 8vo, illustrated boards, 2s. each; cloth limp, 2s. 6d. each.
Cavalry Life. | Regimental Legends.

Cavalry Life and Regimental Legends. LIBRARY EDITION, set in new type and handsomely bound. Crown 8vo, cloth, 3s. 6d.
A Soldier's Children. With 34 Illustrations by E. G. THOMSON and E. STUART HARDY. Crown 8vo, cloth extra, 3s. 6d.

Wissmann (Hermann von). — My Second Journey through Equatorial Africa. With 92 Illustrations. Demy 8vo, cloth, 16s.

Wood (H. F.), Detective Stories by. Post 8vo, boards, 2s. each.
The Passenger from Scotland Yard. | The Englishman of the Rue Cain.

Woolley (Celia Parker).—Rachel Armstrong; or, Love and The-
ology. Post 8vo, illustrated boards, 2s.; cloth, 2s. 6d.

Wright (Thomas), Works by. Crown 8vo, cloth extra, 7s. 6d. each.
The Caricature History of the Georges. With 400 Caricatures, Squibs, &c.
History of Caricature and of the Grotesque in Art, Literature, Sculpture, and
Painting. Illustrated by F. W. FAIRHOLT, F.S.A.

Wynman (Margaret).—My Flirtations. With 13 Illustrations by
J. BERNARD PARTRIDGE. Post 8vo, cloth limp, 2s.

Yates (Edmund), Novels by. Post 8vo, illustrated boards, 2s. each.
Land at Last. | The Forlorn Hope. | Castaway.

Zangwill (I.). — Ghetto Tragedies. With Three Illustrations by
A. S. BOYD. Fcap. 8vo, cloth, 2s. net.

'ZZ.' (Louis Zangwill).—A Nineteenth Century Miracle. Cr.
8vo, cloth, 3s. 6d.

Zola (Emile), Novels by. Crown 8vo, cloth extra, 3s. 6d. each.
The Fortune of the Rougons. Edited by ERNEST A. VIZETELLY.   [Shortly.
The Abbe Mouret's Transgression. Edited by ERNEST A. VIZETELLY.   [Shortly.
His Excellency Eugene Rougon). With an Introduction by ERNEST A. VIZETELLY.
The Dram-Shop (L'Assommoir). With Introduction by E. A. VIZETELLY.
The Fat and the Thin. Translated by ERNEST A. VIZETELLY.
Money. Translated by ERNEST A. VIZETELLY.
The Downfall. Translated by E. A. VIZETELLY.
The Dream. Translated by ELIZA CHASE. With Eight Illustrations by JEANNIOT.
Doctor Pascal. Translated by E. A. VIZETELLY. With Portrait of the Author.
Lourdes. Translated by ERNEST A. VIZETELLY.
Rome. Translated by ERNEST A. VIZETELLY.
Paris. Translated by ERNEST A. VIZETELLY.

SOME BOOKS CLASSIFIED IN SERIES.
₊ For fuller cataloguing, see alphabetical arrangement, pp. 1-26.

The Mayfair Library. Post 8vo, cloth limp, 2s. 6d. per Volume.

A Journey Round My Room. By X. DE MAISTRE.
Translated by Sir HENRY ATTWELL.
Quips and Quiddities. By W. D. ADAMS.
The Agony Column of 'The Times.'
Melancholy Anatomised: Abridgment of BURTON.
Poetical Ingenuities. By W. T. DOBSON.
The Cupboard Papers. By FIN-BEC.
W. S. Gilbert's Plays. Three Series.
Songs of Irish Wit and Humour.
Animals and their Masters. By Sir A HELPS.
Social Pressure. By Sir A. HELPS.
Curiosities of Criticism. By H. J. JENNINGS.
The Autocrat of the Breakfast Table. By OLIVER
WENDELL HOLMES.
Pencil and Palette. By R. KEMPT.
Little Essays: from LAMB'S LETTERS.
Forensic Anecdotes. By JACOB LARWOOD.

Theatrical Anecdotes. By JACOB LARWOOD.
Witch Stories. By E. LYNN LINTON.
Ourselves. By E. LYNN LINTON.
Pastimes and Players. By R. MACGREGOR.
New Paul and Virginia. By W. H. MALLOCK.
The New Republic. By W. H. MALLOCK.
Puck on Pegasus. By H. C. PENNELL.
Pegasus Re-saddled. By H. C. PENNELL.
Muses of Mayfair. Edited by H. C. PENNELL.
Thoreau: His Life and Aims. By H. A. PAGE.
Puniana. By Hon. HUGH ROWLEY.
More Puniana. By Hon. HUGH ROWLEY.
The Philosophy of Handwriting.
By Stream and Sea. By WILLIAM SENIOR.
Leaves from a Naturalist's Note-Book. By Dr.
ANDREW WILSON.

The Golden Library. Post 8vo, cloth limp, 2s. per Volume.

Diversions of the Echo Club. BAYARD TAYLOR.
Songs for Sailors. By W. C. BENNETT.
Lives of the Necromancers. By W. GODWIN.
The Poetical Works of Alexander Pope.
Scenes of Country Life. By EDWARD JESSE.
Tale for a Chimney Corner. By LEIGH HUNT.

The Autocrat of the Breakfast Table. By
OLIVER WENDELL HOLMES.
La Mort d'Arthur: Selections from MALLORY.
Provincial Letters of Blaise Pascal.
Maxims and Reflections of Rochefoucauld.

Handy Novels. Fcap. 8vo, cloth boards, 1s. 6d. each.

The Old Maid's Sweetheart. By A. ST. AUBYN.
Modest Little Sara. By ALAN ST. AUBYN.
Seven Sleepers of Ephesus. M. E. COLERIDGE.
Taken from the Enemy. By H. NEWBOLT.

A Lost Soul. By W. L. ALDEN.
Dr. Palliser's Patient. By GRANT ALLEN.
Monte Carlo Stories. By JOAN BARRETT.
Black Spirits and White. By R. A. CRAM.

My Library. Printed on laid paper, post 8vo, half-Roxburghe, 2s. 6d. each.

Citation and Examination of William Shakspeare.
By W. S. LANDOR.
The Journal of Maurice de Guerin.

Christie Johnstone. By CHARLES READE.
Peg Woffington. By CHARLES READE.
The Dramatic Essays of Charles Lamb.

The Pocket Library. Post 8vo, printed on laid paper and hf.-bd., 2s. each.

The Essays of Elia. By CHARLES LAMB.
Robinson Crusoe. Illustrated by G. CRUIKSHANK.
Whims and Oddities. By THOMAS HOOD.
The Barber's Chair. By DOUGLAS JERROLD.
Gastronomy. By BRILLAT-SAVARIN.
The Epicurean, &c. By THOMAS MOORE.
Leigh Hunt's Essays. Edited by E. OLLIER.

White's Natural History of Selborne.
Gulliver's Travels, &c. By Dean SWIFT.
Plays by RICHARD BRINSLEY SHERIDAN.
Anecdotes of the Clergy. By JACOB LARWOOD.
Thomson's Seasons. Illustrated.
Autocrat of the Breakfast Table and The Professor
at the Breakfast Table. By O. W. HOLMES.

THE PICCADILLY NOVELS.

LIBRARY EDITIONS OF NOVELS, many Illustrated, crown 8vo, cloth extra, 3s. 6d. each.

By Mrs. ALEXANDER.
A Life Interest | Mona's Choice | By Woman's Wit

By F. M. ALLEN.
Green as Grass.

By GRANT ALLEN.
Philistia.
Strange Stories.
Babylon.
For Maimie's Sake,
In all Shades.
The Beckoning Hand.
The Devil's Die.
This Mortal Coil.
The Tents of Shem.

The Great Taboo.
Dumaresq's Daughter.
Duchess of Powysland.
Blood Royal.
Ivan Greet's Masterpiece.
The Scallywag.
At Market Value.
Under Sealed Orders.

By MARY ANDERSON.
Othello's Occupation.

By EDWIN L. ARNOLD.
Phra the Phœnician. | Constable of St. Nicholas.

By ROBERT BARR.
In a Steamer Chair. | A Woman Intervenes.
From Whose Bourne. | Revenge !

By FRANK BARRETT.
The Woman of the Iron Bracelets.
The Harding Scandal. | A Missing Witness.

By 'BELLE.'
Vashti and Esther.

By Sir W. BESANT and J. RICE.
Ready-Money Mortiboy. | By Celia's Arbour.
My Little Girl. | Chaplain of the Fleet.
With Harp and Crown. | The Seamy Side.
This Son of Vulcan. | The Case of Mr. Lucraft.
The Golden Butterfly. | In Trafalgar's Bay.
The Monks of Thelema. | The Ten Years' Tenant.

By Sir WALTER BESANT.
All Sorts and Conditions of Men.
The Captains' Room.
All in a Garden Fair.
Dorothy Forster.
Uncle Jack.
The World Went Very Well Then.
Children of Gibeon.
Herr Paulus.
For Faith and Freedom.
To Call Her Mine.
The Revolt of Man.

The Bell of St. Paul's.
The Holy Rose.
Armorel of Lyonesse.
S.Katherine's by Tower
Verbena Camellia Stephanotis.
The Ivory Gate.
The Rebel Queen.
Beyond the Dreams of Avarice.
The Master Craftsman.
The City of Refuge.

By AMBROSE BIERCE.
In the Midst of Life.

By PAUL BOURGET.
A Living Lie.

By ROBERT BUCHANAN.
Shadow of the Sword.
A Child of Nature.
God and the Man.
Martyrdom of Madeline
Love Me for Ever.
Annan Water.
Foxglove Manor.

The New Abelard.
Matt. | Rachel Dene.
Master of the Mine.
The Heir of Linne.
Woman and the Man.
Red and White Heather.
Lady Kilpatrick.

ROB. BUCHANAN & HY. MURRAY.
The Charlatan.

By J. MITCHELL CHAPPLE.
The Minor Chord.

By HALL CAINE.
The Shadow of a Crime. | The Deemster.
A Son of Hagar.

By ANNE COATES

By MORT. & FRANCES COLLINS.
Transmigration. | From Midnight to Midnight.
Blacksmith & Scholar. |
The Village Comedy. | You Play me False.

By MACLAREN COBBAN.
The Red Sultan. | The Burden of Isabel.

By E. H. COOPER.
Geoffory Hamilton.

By V. CECIL COTES.
Two Girls on a Barge.

By C. EGBERT CRADDOCK.
His Vanished Star.

By H. N. CRELLIN.
Romances of the Old Seraglio.

By MATT CRIM.
The Adventures of a Fair Rebel.

By S. R. CROCKETT and others.
Tales of Our Coast.

By B. M. CROKER.
Diana Barrington.
Proper Pride.
A Family Likeness.
Pretty Miss Neville.
A Bird of Passage.
'To Let.' | Mr. Jervis.
Village Tales & Jungle Tragedies.

The Real Lady Hilda.
Married or Single ?
Two Masters.
In the Kingdom of Kerry
Interference.
A Third Person.

By WILLIAM CYPLES.
Hearts of Gold.

By ALPHONSE DAUDET.
The Evangelist ; or, Port Salvation.

By H. COLEMAN DAVIDSON.
Mr. Sadler's Daughters.

By ERASMUS DAWSON.
The Fountain of Youth.

By JAMES DE MILLE.
A Castle in Spain.

By. J. LEITH DERWENT.
Our Lady of Tears. | Circe's Lovers.

By DICK DONOVAN.
Tracked to Doom. | The Mystery of Jamaica
Man from Manchester. | Terrace.
The Chronicles of Michael Danevitch.

By RICHARD DOWLING.
Old Corcoran's Money.

By A. CONAN DOYLE.
The Firm of Girdlestone.

By S. JEANNETTE DUNCAN.
A Daughter of To-day. | Vernon's Aunt.

By G. MANVILLE FENN.
The New Mistress. | The Tiger Lily.
Witness to the Deed. | The White Virgin.

By PERCY FITZGERALD.
Fatal Zero.

By R. E. FRANCILLON.
One by One. | Ropes of Sand.
A Dog and his Shadow. | Jack Doyle's Daughter.
A Real Queen.

By HAROLD FREDERIC.
Seth's Brother's Wife. | The Lawton Girl.
Prefaced by Sir BARTLE FRERE.
Pandurang Hari.

By PAUL GAULOT.

THE PICCADILLY (3/6) NOVELS—*continued.*

By SYDNEY GRUNDY.
The Days of his Vanity.

By OWEN HALL.
The Track of a Storm. | Jetsam.

By THOMAS HARDY.
Under the Greenwood Tree.

By BRET HARTE.
A Waif of the Plains. | A Protégée of Jack
A Ward of the Golden | Hamlin's.
Gate.   [Springs. | Clarence.
A Sappho of Green | Barker's Luck.
Col. Starbottle's Client. | Devil's Ford.   [celsior.'
Susy. | Sally Dows. | The Crusade of the 'Ex-
Bell-Ringer of Angel's. | Three Partners.
Tales of Trail and Town.

By JULIAN HAWTHORNE.
Garth. | Beatrix Randolph.
Ellice Quentin. | David Poindexter's Dis-
Sebastian Strome. | appearance.
Dust. | The Spectre of the
Fortune's Fool. | Camera.

By Sir A. HELPS.
Ivan de Biron.

By I. HENDERSON.
Agatha Page.

By G. A. HENTY.
Rujub the Juggler. | The Queen's Cup.
Dorothy's Double.

By JOHN HILL.
The Common Ancestor.

By TIGHE HOPKINS.
'Twixt Love and Duty.

By Mrs. HUNGERFORD.
Lady Verner's Flight. | Nora Creina.
The Red-House Mystery | An Anxious Moment.
The Three Graces. | April's Lady.
Professor's Experiment. | Peter's Wife.
A Point of Conscience.

By Mrs. ALFRED HUNT.
The Leaden Casket. | Self-Condemned.
That Other Person. | Mrs. Juliet.

By C. J. CUTCLIFFE HYNE.
Honour of Thieves.

By EDMOND LEPELLETIER.
Madame Sans-Gêne.

By HARRY LINDSAY.
Rhoda Roberts.

By HENRY W. LUCY.
Gideon Fleyce.

By E. LYNN LINTON.
Patricia Kemball. | The Atonement of Leam
Under which Lord? | Dundas.
'My Love!' | Ione. | The World Well Lost.
Paston Carew. | The One Too Many.
Sowing the Wind. | Dulcie Everton.

By JUSTIN McCARTHY.
A Fair Saxon. | Donna Quixote.
Linley Rochford. | Maid of Athens.
Dear Lady Disdain. | The Comet of a Season.
Camiola. | The Dictator.
Waterdale Neighbours. | Red Diamonds.
My Enemy's Daughter. | The Riddle Ring.
Miss Misanthrope. | The Three Disgraces.

By JUSTIN H. McCARTHY.
A London Legend. | The Royal Christopher.

By GEORGE MACDONALD.
Heather and Snow. | Phantastes.

By J. E. MUDDOCK.
Maid Marian and Robin Hood.
Basile the Jester. | Young Lochinvar.

By D. CHRISTIE MURRAY.
A Life's Atonement. | Cynic Fortune.
Joseph's Coat. | The Way of the World.
Coals of Fire. | Bob Martin's Little Girl.
Old Blazer's Hero. | Time's Revenges.
Val Strange. | Hearts. | A Wasted Crime.
A Model Father. | In Direst Peril.
By the Gate of the Sea. | Mount Despair.
A Bit of Human Nature. | A Capful o' Nal's.
First Person Singular. | Tales and Poems.

By MURRAY and HERMAN.
The Bishops' Bible. | Paul Jones's Alias.
One Traveller Returns. |

By HUME NISBET.
'Bail Up!'

By W. E. NORRIS.
Saint Ann's. | Billy Bellew.

By G. OHNET.
A Weird Gift.

By Mrs. OLIPHANT.
The Sorceress.

By OUIDA.
Held in Bondage. | Two Little Wooden
Strathmore. | In a Winter City. [Shoes
Chandos. | Friendship.
Under Two Flags. | Moths. | Ruffino.
Idalia. | [Gage. | Pipistrello.
Cecil Castlemaine's | A Village Commune.
Tricotrin. | Puck. | Bimbi. | Wanda.
Folle Farine. | Frescoes. | Othmar.
A Dog of Flanders. | In Maremma.
Pascarel. | Signa. | Syrlin. | Guilderoy.
Princess Napraxine. | Santa Barbara.
Ariadne. | Two Offenders.

By MARGARET A. PAUL.
Gentle and Simple.

By JAMES PAYN.
Lost Sir Massingberd. | High Spirits.
Less Black than We're | Under One Roof.
Painted. | The Talk of the Town.
A Confidential Agent. | Holiday Tasks.
A Grape from a Thorn. | For Cash Only.
In Peril and Privation. | The Burnt Million.
The Mystery of Mir- | The Word and the Will.
By Proxy. | [bridge. | Sunny Stories.
The Canon's Ward. | A Trying Patient.
Walter's Word. |

By WILL PAYNE.
Jerry the Dreamer.

By Mrs. CAMPBELL PRAED.
Outlaw and Lawmaker. | Mrs. Tregaskiss.
Christina Chard.

By E. C. PRICE.
Valentina. | Foreigners. | Mrs. Lancaster's Rival.

By RICHARD PRYCE.
Miss Maxwell's Affections.

By CHARLES READE.
Peg Woffington; and | Love Me Little, Love
Christie Johnstone. | Me Long.
Hard Cash. | The Double Marriage.
Cloister & the Hearth. | Foul Play.
Never Too Late to Mend | Put Yourself in His
The Course of True | Place.
Love Never Did Run | A Terrible Temptation.

THE PICCADILLY (3/6) NOVELS—*continued.*

By W. CLARK RUSSELL.

Round the Galley-Fire.
In the Middle Watch.
On the Fo'k'sle Head.
A Voyage to the Cape.
Bock for the Hammock.
Mystery of 'Ocean Star'
The Romance of Jenny Harlowe.
An Ocean Tragedy.

My Shipmate Louise.
Alone on Wide Wide Sea.
The Phantom Death.
Is He the Man?
Good Ship 'Mohock.'
The Convict Ship.
Heart of Oak.
The Tale of the Ten.
The Last Entry.

By DORA RUSSELL.
A Country Sweetheart. | The Drift of Fate.

By HERBERT RUSSELL.
True Blue.

By BAYLE ST. JOHN.
A Levantine Family.

By ADELINE SERGEANT.
Dr. Endicott's Experiment.

By HAWLEY SMART.
Without Love or Licence. | The Outsider.
The Master of Rathkelly. | Beatrice & Benedick.
Long Odds. | A Racing Rubber.

By T. W. SPEIGHT.
A Secret of the Sea. | A Minion of the Moon.
The Grey Monk. | The Secret of Wyvern
The Master of Trenance | Towers.

By ALAN ST. AUBYN.
A Fellow of Trinity. | In Face of the World.
The Junior Dean. | Orchard Damerel.
Master of St. Benedict's. | The Tremlett Diamonds.
To his Own Master.

By JOHN STAFFORD.
Doris and I.

By RICCARDO STEPHENS.
The Cruciform Mark.

By R. A. STERNDALE.
The Afghan Knife.

By R. LOUIS STEVENSON.
The Suicide Club.

By BERTHA THOMAS.
Proud Maisie. | The Violin-Player.

By ANTHONY TROLLOPE.
The Way we Live Now. | Scarborough's Family.
Fran Frohmann. | The Land-Leaguers

By FRANCES E. TROLLOPE.
Like Ships upon the Sea. | Anne Furness.
| Mabel's Progress.

By IVAN TURGENIEFF, &c.
Stories from Foreign Novelists.

By MARK TWAIN.
Mark Twain's Choice Works.
Mark Twain's Library of Humour.
The Innocents Abroad.
Roughing It; and The Innocents at Home.
A Tramp Abroad.
The American Claimant.
Adventures Tom Sawyer
Tom Sawyer Abroad.

Tom Sawyer, Detective.
Pudd'nhead Wilson.
The Gilded Age.
Prince and the Pauper.
Life on the Mississippi.
The Adventures of Huckleberry Finn.
A Yankee at the Court of King Arthur.
Stolen White Elephant.
£1,000,000 Banknote.

By C. C. FRASER-TYTLER.
Mistress Judith.

By SARAH TYTLER.
Lady Bell.
Buried Diamonds.
The Blackhall Ghosts.

The Macdonald Lass.
The Witch-Wife.

By ALLEN UPWARD.
The Queen against Owen | The Prince of Balkistan.

By E. A. VIZETELLY.
The Scorpion : A Romance of Spain.

By CY WARMAN.
The Express Messenger.

By WILLIAM WESTALL.
Sons of Belial.

By ATHA WESTBURY.
The Shadow of Hilton Fernbrook.

By C. J. WILLS.
An Easy-going Fellow.

By JOHN STRANGE WINTER.
Cavalry Life and Regimental Legends.
A Soldier's Children.

By MARGARET WYNMAN.
My Flirtations.

By E. ZOLA.
The Fortune of the Rougons.
The Abbe Mouret's Transgression.
The Downfall.
The Dream.
Dr. Pascal.
Money. | Lourdes.

The Fat and the Thin.
His Excellency.
The Dram-Shop.
Rome. | Paris.

By 'Z Z.'
A Nineteenth Century Miracle.

CHEAP EDITIONS OF POPULAR NOVELS.

Post 8vo, illustrated boards, 2s. each.

By ARTEMUS WARD.
Artemus Ward Complete.

By EDMOND ABOUT.
The Fellah.

By HAMILTON AÏDÉ.
Carr of Carrlyon. | Confidences.

By Mrs. ALEXANDER.
Maid, Wife, or Widow? | A Life Interest.
Blind Fate. | Mona's Choice.
Valerie's Fate. | By Woman's Wit.

By GRANT ALLEN.
Philistia. | Babylon.
Strange Stories.
For Maimie's Sake.
In all Shades.
The Beckoning Hand.
The Devil's Die.
The Tents of Shem.
The Great Taboo.

Dumaresq's Daughter.
Duchess of Powysland.
Blood Royal. [piece-
Ivan Greet's Master.
The Scallywag.
This Mortal Coil.
At Market Value.
Under Sealed Orders.

By E. LESTER ARNOLD.
Phra the Phœnician.

BY FRANK BARRETT.
Fettered for Life.
Little Lady Linton.
Between Life & Death.
Sin of Olga Zassoulich.
Folly Morrison.
Lieut. Barnabas.

A Prodigal's Progress.
Found Guilty.
A Recoiling Vengeance.
For Love and Honour.
John Ford, &c.
Woman of Iron Brace'ts

By SHELSLEY BEAUCHAMP.
Grantley Grange.

By Sir W. BESANT and J. RICE.
Ready-Money Mortiboy
My Little Girl.
With Harp and Crown.
This Son of Vulcan.
The Golden Butterfly.
The Monks of Thelema.

By Celia's Arbour.
Chaplain of the Fleet.
The Seamy Side.
The Case of Mr. Lucraft.
In Trafalgar's Bay.
The Ten Years' Tenant.

By Sir WALTER BESANT.
All Sorts and Conditions of Men.
The Captains' Room.
All in a Garden Fair.
Dorothy Forster.
Uncle Jack.
The World Went Very Well Then.
Children of Gibeon.
Herr Paulus.
For Faith and Freedom.
To Call Her Mine.

The Bell of St. Paul's.
The Holy Rose.
Armorel of Lyonesse.
S. Katherine's by Tower.
Verbena Camellia Stephanotis.
The Ivory Gate.
The Rebel Queen.
Beyond the Dreams of Avarice.
The Revolt of Man.
In Deacon's Orders.

By AMBROSE BIERCE.
In the Midst of Life.

By FREDERICK BOYLE.
Camp Notes.
Savage Life.

Chronicles of No man's Land.

BY BRET HARTE.
Californian Stories.
Gabriel Conroy.
Luck of Roaring Camp.

Flip. | Maruja.
A Phyllis of the Sierras.
A Waif of the Plains.

Two-Shilling Novels—*continued.*

By JAMES PAYN.

Bentinck's Tutor.
Murphy's Master.
A County Family.
At Her Mercy.
Cecil's Tryst.
The Clyffards of Clyffe.
The Foster Brothers.
Found Dead.
The Best of Husbands.
Walter's Word
Halves.
Fallen Fortunes.
Humorous Stories.
£200 Reward.
A Marine Residence.
Mirk Abbey
By Proxy.
Under One Roof.
High Spirits.
Carlyon's Year.
From Exile.
For Cash Only.
Kit.
The Canon's Ward.

The Talk of the Town.
Holiday Tasks.
A Perfect Treasure.
What He Cost Her.
A Confidential Agent.
Glow-worm Tales.
The Burnt Million.
Sunny Stories.
Lost Sir Massingberd.
A Woman's Vengeance.
The Family Scapegrace.
Gwendoline's Harvest.
Like Father, Like Son.
Married Beneath Him.
Not Wooed, but Won.
Less Black than We're Painted.
Some Private Views.
A Grape from a Thorn.
The Mystery of Mirbridge.
The Word and the Will.
A Prince of the Blood.
A Trying Patient.

By CHARLES READE.

It is Never Too Late to Mend.
Christie Johnstone.
The Double Marriage.
Put Yourself in His Place
Love Me Little, Love Me Long.
The Cloister and the Hearth.
The Course of True Love.
The Jilt.
The Autobiography of a Thief.

A Terrible Temptation.
Foul Play.
The Wandering Heir.
Hard Cash.
Singleheart and Doubleface.
Good Stories of Man and other Animals.
Peg Woffington.
Griffith Gaunt.
A Perilous Secret.
A Simpleton.
Readiana.
A Woman-Hater.

By Mrs. J. H. RIDDELL.

Weird Stories.
Fairy Water.
Her Mother's Darling.
The Prince of Wales's Garden Party.

The Uninhabited House.
The Mystery in Palace Gardens.
The Nun's Curse.
Idle Tales.

By AMELIE RIVES.

Barbara Dering.

By F. W. ROBINSON.

Women are Strange.
The Hands of Justice.

The Woman in the Dark

By JAMES RUNCIMAN.

Skippers and Shellbacks. | Schools and Scholars.
Grace Balmaign's Sweetheart.

By W. CLARK RUSSELL.

Round the Galley Fire.
On the Fo'k'sle Head.
In the Middle Watch.
A Voyage to the Cape.
A Book for the Hammock.
The Mystery of the 'Ocean Star.'
The Romance of Jenny Harlowe.

An Ocean Tragedy.
My Shipmate Louise.
Alone on Wide Wide Sea.
The Good Ship 'Mohock.'
The Phantom Death.
Is He the Man.
Heart of Oak.
The Convict Ship.

By DORA RUSSELL.

A Country Sweetheart.

By GEORGE AUGUSTUS SALA.

Gaslight and Daylight.

By GEORGE R. SIMS.

The Ring o' Bells.
Mary Jane's Memoirs.
Mary Jane Married.
Tales of To-day.
Dramas of Life.
Tinkletop's Crime.
My Two Wives.

Zeph.
Memoirs of a Landlady.
Scenes from the Show.
The 10 Commandments.
Dagonet Abroad.
Rogues and Vagabonds.

By ARTHUR SKETCHLEY.

A Match in the Dark.

By HAWLEY SMART.

Without Love or Licence. | The Plunger.
Beatrice and Benedick. | Long Odds.
The Master of Rathkelly. |

By T. W. SPEIGHT.

The Mysteries of Heron Dyke.
The Golden Hoop.
Hoodwinked.
By Devious Ways.

Back to Life.
The Londwater Tragedy.
Burgo's Romance.
Quittance in Full.
A Husband from the Sea

By ALAN ST. AUBYN.

A Fellow of Trinity.
The Junior Dean.
Master of St. Benedict's
To His Own Master.

Orchard Damerel.
In the Face of the World.
The Tremlett Diamonds.

By R. A. STERNDALE.

The Afghan Knife.

By R. LOUIS STEVENSON.

New Arabian Nights.

By BERTHA THOMAS.

Cressida. | The Violin-Player.
Proud Maisie. |

By WALTER THORNBURY.

Tales for the Marines. | Old Stories Retold.

By T. ADOLPHUS TROLLOPE.

Diamond Cut Diamond.

By F. ELEANOR TROLLOPE.

Like Ships upon the Sea.
Anne Furness.
Mabel's Progress.

By ANTHONY TROLLOPE.

Frau Frohmann.
Marion Fay.
Kept in the Dark.
John Caldigate.
The Way We Live Now.

The Land-Leaguers.
The American Senator.
Mr. Scarborough's Family.
Golden Lion of Granpere

By J. T. TROWBRIDGE.

Farnell's Folly.

By IVAN TURGENIEFF, &c.

Stories from Foreign Novelists.

By MARK TWAIN.

A Pleasure Trip on the Continent.
The Gilded Age.
Huckleberry Finn.
Mark Twain's Sketches.
Tom Sawyer.
A Tramp Abroad.
Stolen White Elephant.

Life on the Mississippi.
The Prince and the Pauper.
A Yankee at the Court of King Arthur.
The £1,000,000 Bank-Note.

By C. C. FRASER-TYTLER.

Mistress Judith.

By SARAH TYTLER.

The Bride's Pass.
Buried Diamonds.
St. Mungo's City.
Lady Bell.
Noblesse Oblige.
Disappeared.

The Huguenot Family.
The Blackhall Ghosts.
What She Came Through
Beauty and the Beast.
Citoyenne Jaqueline.

By ALLEN UPWARD.

The Queen against Owen. | Prince of Balkistan.
'God Save the Queen!'

By AARON WATSON and LILLIAS WASSERMANN.

The Marquis of Carabas.

By WILLIAM WESTALL.

Trust-Money.

By Mrs. F. H. WILLIAMSON.

A Child Widow.

By J. S. WINTER.

Cavalry Life. | Regimental Legends.

By H. F. WOOD.

The Passenger from Scotland Yard.
The Englishman of the Rue Cain.

By CELIA PARKER WOOLLEY.

Rachel Armstrong; or, Love and Theology.

By EDMUND YATES.

The Forlorn Hope. | Castaway.
Land at Last. |

By I. ZANGWILL.

Ghetto Tragedies.